Our
Cosmic
Dance

Our Cosmic Dance

AN AUTOBIOGRAPHY OF COURAGE, FAITH, AND SPIRITUAL TRIUMPH

Moreah Ragusa

Phoenix ©
Coaching and Transformation Corporation

Published by The Phoenix Coaching and Transformation Corporation
Calgary, Alberta, Canada

Library and Archives Canada Cataloguing in Publication

Ragusa, Moreah
  Our cosmic dance : an autobiography of courage, faith, and spiritual triumph / Moreah Ragusa.

ISBN 978-0-7795-0079-6

  I. Ragusa, Moreah. 2. Self-actualization (Psychology) 3. Interpersonal relations. 4. Spiritual biography—Canada. I. Phoenix Coaching and Transformation Corp. II. Title.

BF637.S4R334 2007   I58.I   C2007-907141-4

Cover design by Shelley Hedges
Text design and layout by Heidy Lawrance, HLAcreative.com
Author photo by Carolyn Sandstrom

Inquiries, orders, and other requests should be addressed to:
The Phoenix Coaching and Transformation Corporation
11550 – 44 Street SE, Calgary, Alberta, Canada T2Z 4A2
Phone: 403-278-3700
E-mail: info@thephoenixcoaching.com
www.moreah.ca

*This book is lovingly dedicated to those
I have danced with and loved.*

Moreah Ragusa

Contents

PART THREE

Preface

Each and every one of us has a crucial role to play in the Cosmic Dance. You might as well learn the steps, so that you can shine on the dance floor of your life. Sometimes, your dance partner is a person. Other times, it's a particular situation that is designed to etch upon your soul the knowledge of your strengths and, sometimes, your deepest fears. Nevertheless, the Cosmic Dance in which you are a partner has never, nor will it ever, be danced by anyone but you. It is sacred. The whole universe, of which you are an integral part, orchestrates the people and events that have the highest learning potential for you–the potential to reveal your brilliance and your capacity to love–unconditionally.

By conscious design, you and your nonphysical teachers have imposed filters on your psyche–archetypes. These archetypes are culminations of traits, such as nurturing, dominance, gentleness, aggression, dishonesty, and cowering. The components of particular traits become a pattern of influence or "character." These characters have been written about through the ages in fairy tails and mythologies of various kinds. Dominant traits that are expressing through the personality become filters through which we can learn about our soul and the nature of the Creator or Source from which all things come, and disappear into. These filters show up as archetypal paradigms, such as the *Warrior, Saboteur, Mother, Lover,* or *Victim.* These archetypes are neutral and impersonal, and are designed to work as aids in uncovering what blocks us from expressing and appreciating love. In our limited awareness, we are both polarizing (experiencing as positive or negative) and uniquely personalizing these patterns to reveal our Cosmic Dance.

Your life is your dance floor, the experiences are the dances, and each person that is in your life, or has been and will be in it, is a dance partner designed to teach you how to love and become fully human, fully actualized, and aware that you are a cosmic citizen of unmentionable worth. My life is my dance floor, too, and the people and events that I have "danced" with have taught me that there is an organizing power that is deeply invested in my knowing who I am. It is my sincerest wish that by sharing with you the story of my dances and some of my partners, I will encourage you to embrace your dance, too!

*I*ntroduction

Whenever we see a master performing in their particular discipline—their dance—we are awed by the ease with which they perform tasks that, if we were to do them, would make us look inadequate or handicapped. In fact, one of the distinguishing factors I have in identifying a master in any area of life, is when they can make their action or performance look as easy as something that even a toddler could do. The easier they make their skill appear, the more masterful they are.

Each of us is a master also, and we each have an art—something we can do so brilliantly that to observing eyes, we make that "art" appear effortless. Just as any master, we are also able to excel at our specialty because we have seen all sides and are aware of all the inherent problems and solutions. It is this magnified and detailed understanding that gives us mastery in it. Masters see their specialty like a magnet. It needs two opposing sides, so that they can dance in the middle. Masters are skilled at stabilizing the light and dark, high and low, seen and unseen, so that both comedy and tragedy can move through their life.

Mastery comes from knowing and appreciating both sides of anything. Masters know that in order to reveal their brilliance and competence in their arena, two equal and opposing sides are vital. These pairs of opposites are bedfellows for life. For the magician, it is mastery in the known and unknown—the truth and illusion, dark and light, and the danger and safety that inspire us to awe.

In addition, the master tightrope walker, for instance, knows that the height and inherent danger of falling off the rope are essential ingredients to her gaining mastery in staying balanced on the rope. Masters are not under the illusion that there is only one side to anything—or to anyone. Masters know that it is the unavoidable presence of the equal and opposite sides to anything that makes it real.

Each of us has two sides also—the side or traits that we own, feel proud of, and appreciate, and the equal and opposite side or traits we often despise, hide, and view as evil and thus disown. The side we shine light on is our perceived positive or good side, because we do not stop to consider that some of the traits that we see as positive also produce negative results. Likewise, the traits we have that we view as negative have often not been contemplated long enough to allow us to see the positives they induce.

In reality, we are as magnets with two sides—the positive and the negative both are necessary and inseparable. The master is therefore not trying to eliminate one side—rather he or she is embracing, appreciating, and transforming eternally. In other words, he or she is self-actualizing. The dances we are here to dance are really just opportunities to learn how to appreciate both sides, of one another and of ourselves. The embracing of the two sides is to love —unconditionally.

We will never get rid of one of our sides, nor should we desire to do so. We will always have peace and war, hot and cold, up and down, mean and nice, darkness and light!

Because these traits always come as inseparable pairs, we

will never in reality have one side touching our life, either. At the moment that someone is nice, we will also be experiencing someone being mean. Sometimes we are that someone! Admittedly, to look for the opposite side is not something we have been trained to do, but if we want to live masterfully, and finally recognize that love is unbounded, omnipotent, and omniscient, it is crucial that we do.

In the stories that I will share with you, it is important that you understand that I do not view (perceive) my life to be anything but a magnificent dance. I have come to recognize that three divine influences, or deities, have attended my every step. These three deities have always guided the human evolutionary process. Their function is to teach us that there is an implicit ordering intelligence moving through us and through our lives. The deities of *Necessity*, *Compassion*, and *Choice* have, in their turn, guided me to discover the innate order that is in constant presence, even though at times I could not see or understand it.

Necessity helps us to understand that certain people were "contracted" by us to teach us how to love. *Compassion* urges us to act through a filter that asks, "Do unto others only as you would want to have it done unto you." Choice encourages us to act from our authentic self—it always asks us to make a choice from our highest potential. Choice nudges us to consider what motivates our choices: truth or lies, fear or love. We may have to break free of limiting concepts of self in order to make the choice that is most congruent with our true nature.

Our three companions are ever encouraging us to look at our life as an opportunity to dance with our global siblings in order that we might know and love ourselves more fully.

Being aware of this, I have looked with an open and honest heart and mind to review circumstances and experiences that one would traditionally perceive as "bad" or even "tragic" that have touched my life. I have discovered that for every "bad," there was a "good" or "spectacular" that simultaneously and miraculously occurred.

As my friend Dr. John Demartini has so often stated, we should all consider a coin, which has two sides—a heads and a tails side—each representing the good and bad, but if we want to have the coin, we must take both sides in order to have it. The coin itself is love.

My life experiences encompassed two sides also; and in the middle of the two opposing sides, open for me to embrace, was love. The experience itself was my opportunity to become a master and learn how to dance.

It is from that great discovery that I have found the gratitude and wisdom to share my dance with you—the knowing that in each and every instant I had both pleasure and pain—has birthed a "mindful" recognition that my life has been bathed in, and attended by, love. Mine is a life that I would not change and one that I am deeply grateful for.

Part One

Things don't change.
You change your way of looking, that's all.

Carlos Castaneda

CHAPTER I

Parental Dance Partners

DANCE PARTNER ONE

My first dance partner was my dad. One day while meditating, I suddenly realized that I had gone back in time–I was with my dad, but not really. Strangely enough, I was with him yet not in a physical form–I just was. He was much younger, and he had a magical spark about him. I hovered around, apparently awaiting my first dance.

Suddenly, I felt myself racing and reaching, swaying and grasping, but for what, I wondered. One part of me did not need to understand for what, while another part knew. Magnetically powered it seemed; I just needed to swim, and surge forward!

All this occurred while I was simultaneously observing some form of myself race for a finish line that strangely appeared to be another form of me. The other form was a transparent island that I absolutely had to reach. My success would determine if I were to dance on earth now. I suppose the island was an ovum; and, strange as it seems, the ovum was both my mom and I. Then, suddenly, I became aware of my need to dance differently; this time with my second dance partner, my mom.

Magically, my father was handing me off so Mom and I could engage in our nine-month dance—a dance that transformed energy into matter, light into form. Actually, the dance lasted for 37.5 weeks, and on October 9, 1964, in Genoa, Italy, I placed my tiny slipperless feet upon the dance floor of my earthbound life.

My earliest memories of my mom's indiscreet ways of giving me clues that I had an earnest desire to live was of her often repeating, "By all scientific and medical accounts, you were supposed to die." My medical problem was due to an incompatibility of parental blood rhesus factors that required repeated blood transfusions while I was an infant. Mom would then continue by reminding me of her equally strong commitment to saving my life by giving up chocolate for seven years as a bargain with God if he would keep me alive. This initial life challenge would prove to be the first of many more tests of my determination to live.

Certainty was needed, on my part, if I was to remain dancing. Without question, I was being taught early on about the incredible power of *Choice*, *Certainty*, and *Necessity*, but, most of all, about the dynamics of love and that love was really the synthesizing of opposing sides, or forces.

When I work with individuals, I sometimes come across people who question their right to life. These individuals have felt this way since their embryonic stage in utero, with differing components that left them wondering if they were worthy of living. For some individuals, the parental dynamics had a significant impact, while for others it was the absence or death of a family member. Others seemed to be greatly impacted by their mothers' or fathers' either not wanting them or wanting a baby of a different sex.

One of my daughters is among those souls who, from the onset, felt unworthy and unwanted. I will discuss her story at length in a subsequent chapter, but for now let's consider why some souls feel so unworthy of living. All souls are here learning two primary lessons. One is the integration of being, through learning how to be grateful for all parts and traits of themselves—a basic self-esteem lesson, and the second is the deepest learning of the meaning of love. However, because we are so addicted to a fantasy version of love, depression or suicidal thoughts are unavoidable until we become willing to examine the downside of the fantasy.

As a society, we need to redefine what life and living means. Collectively, we need to acknowledge that we tend to see the world with one eye closed. We have not been taught to look for both sides and realize that neither side is better—just that both are necessary. Nor have we been taught to realize that, since energy cannot be created or destroyed, we need only look for the new form of whatever we perceive is missing. Lastly, one of the biggest gifts we give back to ourselves and humanity is the realization that the "form" of what we want may well change, but that the new form is of equal value to the development of the soul.

MOM'S HONOR CODE

My mom was quite a lady, or gypsy, I should say. She was the first to teach me that I could even dance alone, because she had. Gypsies have their own code of ethics, values, and morals—basically a "whatever it takes" honor code. Mom's honor code included taking whatever she needed or wanted, without permission, hesitation, or guilt! She was one of my greatest teachers in educating me that we have two sides, and that both are valuable and lovable. Both sides are necessary and are not to be judged, and neither is better or worse than the other!

As a child, I adored my mom. She was the prettiest, cleverest, and most awesome person I knew, and I deeply wanted to make her happy. However, it seemed to me that she was fighting an invisible war—but with whom or what, I did not know. Nevertheless, I suspected it had something to do with her childhood and my dad. In her eyes, I could see a yearning for a way to ease her perceived childhood pain.

Mom's mother had died when she was three, and although Mom couldn't remember her mother, she grieved for whatever she imagined her to be, and for whatever she thought she was missing. Mom had a single beautifully framed black-and-white photograph of my grandmother that she clung to and cherished in the same way that I cherished Mom.

The fact that her own mother had died when Mom was very young seemed, in her mind, to be an enormous betrayal of life. As a result, she appeared to be always feeling cautious, mistrusting, and overly defensive towards almost everyone who came into her life.

A coping mechanism that helped Mom function in

what she perceived to be a deeply wounded life was the fact that she became a brilliant storyteller. She loved to tell fantastic stories over and over, and it was not until I became a young adult that I figured out that many of the stories were fantasies that had as their aim to make her appear very "special" and better than everyone else.

Interestingly, Mom often told me a story of how at age four, she had pointed out to a housekeeper the gravesite of her mother—even though she had never been taken there. I suppose that it is entirely possible that Mom's psychic ability was highly developed, as is mine. We both felt that our parents were unable to fulfill their traditional roles in our lives. In our respective childhoods, we both learned to turn inward to fill our perceived voids. Guides and teachers from the other side then took the place of parents.

Psychic or intuitive abilities are often heightened as a result of increased need and frequently follow perceived trauma. Thus, they become a coping mechanism. Individuals who felt abandoned or helpless as children, or those who have suffered dramatic losses, often compensate in this way. These people either can't rely on or don't trust the family or the people around them, so they begin to rely on, and get their guidance through, energy information. The mind, which has a self-equilibrating nature, will create images of guides often seen internally as mental pictures in order to allow us to experience both sides of love. Remember that love is the synthesis of two opposing traits or qualities, for instance kind/cruel, up/down, seen/unseen. We will discuss this in more detail in a later chapter.

Mom was a prime example of this dynamic. She often shared a childhood story that she felt made her very "special." Mom proudly stated how often she startled people with the knowledge she intuitively had about the whereabouts of her mother's gravesite. She repeatedly verbalized that her childhood was tumultuous, filled with fear, abandonment, abuse, and a cruel housekeeper that made her peel potatoes all day long. She, like so many of us, looked upon hard times with one eye closed.

Reflecting on this today, I could, if I had the opportunity, invite her to find the other side to the childhood tragedy, so that she could feel the love that I am certain was always there. Having said this, I should mention that my Mom has not been a part of my day-to-day life for the past 20 years. Although she is in my heart, and I still feel deeply connected to her on a spiritual level, it is because of her severe personality disorders and her criminal record that we became separated physically.

In all honesty, then, I can only deduce, based on the personality disorders Mom expressed, that she perceived her childhood to have been quite dreadful. What exactly her experience was I do not know. Gratefully, however, her perceived childhood pain had inspired her to search for the divine, and for the deepest meaning of life. For this I am deeply grateful, and am inspired to follow in her footsteps.

Archetypes and Their Influences

An archetype is the culmination of a set of traits or qualities that together inspire predictable actions. The *Mother* archetype is itself neutral, but can be polarized by lopsided perceptions into the opposing qualities of positive or good, and negative or bad. *Mother* in the positive extreme would be

Mrs Joan Cleaver in the 70s program *Leave It to Beaver*, and in the negative, it would be Joan Crawford in *Mommy Dearest*. In my life, I would by *Necessity* experience both sides of this archetype as polarized until I could see, and love, the benefits of each side. Once I had discovered that *mothering* has and needs two sides, and that both sides together make up a mother's love, I could finally forgive myself, both for the times I had been awful and for the times I had been too soft.

THE ARCHETYPE OF MOTHER PERCEIVED THROUGH A CHILD'S MIND

I was three or four and diapering my baby doll in our Vancouver apartment. Although I did not know it then, the archetype of *Mother* would have a profound impact on the shaping of my soul in this lifetime.

While *mothering* my baby doll, which I loved to do, I was also very busy conversing with my inner teacher, my "little voice." This voice was an inner guide that I can't ever remember being without. On this particular day, I was suddenly *remembering* that I had come, this time, to learn yet a deeper and more real understanding of the true meaning of love.

The "inner voice" confirmed my memory and also reminded me that no matter what, "It" would be with me, guiding and lifting me whenever I asked for help. Somehow, I just knew this life was to teach me more about love than I had learned before. *Mother* as an archetypal pattern had already begun to shape my soul and my understanding of the Deity-Mother God. Compared to the degree that I would understand the two sides of the *Mother* archetype later in life, I was still very naïve and unaware at that time. Through the process of soul evolution, *Necessity* would have me undergo a curriculum that would entail experiences of perceived unspeakable sacrifice, pain, and suffering. I would need to learn the full scope of what the archetype *Mother* can and will do—its shadow and light sides. To come to fully understand the impact of the *Mother* archetype on our spiritual growth, I would need to dance with life itself, and so, it seems, I did.

To love here on earth the way we do "at home" is what I yearned for. But *how* I knew it was different here than "at home," I will not explain—*yet*. I did, however, presume it would be easy to love "that way" here. I still remember feeling a weight of something indescribably mysterious within my heart when thinking that life with love "like that" would be wonderful to give and experience here.

I have since come to know that the weight I felt when I was so young was one that reflected my soul awareness about the essential *curriculum*, the trials and tribulations that were ordered "by *Necessity*" to learn the deeper lessons of a mother's love. In retrospect, I realize that the early years of this life were not meant to be easy; they were meant to be powerful—of that I am certain.

REMEMBERING WHAT SHOULD HAVE BEEN FORGOTTEN

The second fundamental dance step I took occurred when I was five. We regularly traveled back and forth between our suburban home and the city of Vancouver. Traveling along the freeway and counting the lines on the road somehow set powerful inquisitions and memories ablaze within me. Admittedly, these ponderings were not those of the average young child; rather, they were those of a deeply questioning and evolving soul, who had somehow found itself in a foreign land, *without a map*. My memories would literally blow apart my still so young conceptual understanding of who or what I really was...and ignite an insatiable yearning to remember—from where exactly did I come, and why? And, more importantly, why did I feel so alien here?

I distinctly remember feeling overwhelmed and confused when observing my physical surroundings. "This isn't anything like it was the last time I was here... This is not like home... Why do we need all of those buildings...? How did everything get to be like this...? Why does everything look so separate and alone...? What is the point of this place...? Often, I felt, both overwhelmed and "shell-shocked" by it all.

In order to find some comfort, I naturally turned within, and in doing so, a deep knowing that my heavenly parents, known to me as guides, angels, and teachers, were always with me, returned. Any time I turned inward, these feelings magically eased.

Even though "this place" had dramatically changed since my last visit, I knew I had come to *make a difference*, and that I had a purpose—a contract to uphold. How I was to do that I did not yet know, but I knew it was not going to be easy. Somehow, I knew that the "inner voice" did know my contract details, and one day, when I was ready to heed the call, "It" would tell me.

By age 7, I had developed a constant and natural communicative relationship with Jesus. I was first baptized

Catholic, yet in the church and in school, I felt as though others didn't know Jesus the way I did. In essence, I did not idolize or venerate Him, I just hung out with Him—He was my buddy, my friend. Hours passed effortlessly as I played, daydreamed, and conversed with Him anytime I wanted to. No matter where my parents were or how I needed to fend for my brothers or myself, I was really never afraid because I was never really alone.

One day, I began feeling quite guilty for feeling as though I loved Jesus more than God. This had never happened before, and I realize now that it was a marker of my maturing human, rather than spirit, identity. Jesus, to whom I related as to a big brother, felt a lot more "like me" than God did. I suppose it was because I saw Jesus in a human form, and I didn't exactly remember what form God was in. To compensate for the loss of memory of God's appearance, I began embodying Him in a very old body with a white flowing beard—as so many other children did. Regardless of the form, I hoped that God would understand my favoritism towards my brother and "buddy."

Every calling is great, when greatly pursued.

Oliver Wendell Holmes, Jr.

CHAPTER 2

Two-Sided Love

My early childhood was complex and diversified in its dynamics, to say the least. Socially engendered labels that might be used to describe my family life would include alcoholism, abandonment, and mental illness, as well as physical violence involving deadly weapons, verbal abuse, and explosive temperaments. Both my parents' unhealed and unloved selves seemed to dominate our young family unit.

My parents, who had immigrated from Europe in 1968, were desperately struggling in their marriage, and in their relationship to my dad's parents in Italy. According to my dad, he had been "tricked" into marriage. Mom had become pregnant with my brother in 1961 and had threatened my father with taking her life if he wouldn't marry her. My dad believed that, somewhere along their brief dating period, Mom had discovered that he came from a wealthy family. Naturally, then, she concluded that a perfect way to hang on to this fine catch was to turn a sexual fling quickly into marriage via pregnancy.

Dad told me that my grandparents had checked out Mom's family and had discovered that they came from a long line of gypsies. They had also found out that Mom had a history of mental illness. As a result of their findings, my grandparents forbade my father to marry my mother, in spite of their strict Catholic beliefs, which encourage marriage if premarital sex (not permitted in Catholicism) has resulted in pregnancy. My grandparents turned against their own religious beliefs and were willing to negotiate their values in order to achieve the break-up of my parents' relationship and the termination of the pregnancy. This example demonstrates the truth that we are only committed to our highest values and priorities, not to people or institutions. We will either break or bend otherwise self-governing rules when our top values are being challenged. In addition, we will compromise lower-placed values for the top ones if we can see a gain in doing so.

My grandmother, who suspected Mom's hidden motives, warned Dad that if he were to disobey his parents' orders to "get rid of her," he would be excommunicated from the family, and the inheritance. Feeling torn between his parents' wishes and Mom's pregnancy, he needed to decide which choice served his highest values at that time. Apparently, Mom must have offered him more perceived value, since he married her anyway. As he had been warned, Dad was in fact turned out of his family and its resources for several months following his decision.

Then, by a stroke of destiny, Dad's uncle told him that Canadian Pacific Airlines was hiring, and he felt that Dad should apply. He did, was hired, and then stationed in Vancouver, Canada, where he moved the family in 1968 to begin a life of their own–away from parental influences.

The next twelve years would prove to be filled with feelings of coercion, entrapment, and rage for my parents. They both seemed to be at their best when they were apart from each other. Fortunately, because my father was a purser with the airlines, he was away from home a lot. In hindsight, this was probably what kept the marriage going as long as it did.

Dad's Catholic upbringing had instilled the belief that one married only once–that marriage was for life, regardless of how miserable the marriage was. Mom's self-induced dementia and hysteria made Dad's life a living hell. Accusations of affairs, lies, and dishonesty were woven into the fabric of the marriage and our childhood years. For my parents, who felt trapped by religious beliefs and, on Mom's part, by a lack of education and financial resources, depression quickly escalated into rage. Soon after that, weapons and death threats became "normal forms of communication" for my brothers and me to witness our parents partaking in. As children, we knew no different, so this was just our life, our path of love.

Each of us children created ways to have fun, through fantasies and pleasure, to equalize the drama. Each of us had (as all children do) both pleasure and pain in perfect balance, so that we, like all children, regardless of circumstance, had both sides of the coin we can call love. For my older brother, reprieve came from escaping into TV, fantasy worlds with friends, and hours of playing with Lego construction blocks. For me, it was daydreaming about boys, talking with angels and guides, and endless hours of playing with neighbours' children that helped me cope with the fighting I witnessed. For my youngest brother, the dynamics between my parents caused emotional stunting; their fighting left him feeling both helpless and as if he were to blame. I saw in his eyes total confusion, as he so often felt rejected by Mom, and abandoned by Dad. He fared the worst, and sought negative attention to cope. To soften his pain, I often played the role of mother, and my older brother played out the role of father to him.

I could see the pain in both my parents' eyes, and I spent hours trying to make them understand each other, and to find common ground for them to focus on. Frequently, I sought inner guidance from my heavenly teachers to help counsel my parents to some sort of peace and understanding.

Due to the nature of Dad's employment, he would often be gone for weeks at a time. When he was away, there was no fighting, and peace and normalcy were reinstated for the most part. Mom was a softy, and could be easily manipulated by our emotions. Dad was the opposite. Because Mom did not understand that we needed both sides of parenting, and that he was a reflection of her disowned parts, she criticized his character whenever he was away.

Over time, and because of the intensity of Dad's work schedule, the long time periods without him began to estrange him from the family unit altogether. When Mom was bashing Dad in his absence, we quickly learned to take her side. We were her life, and she did not want to share our love or us with anyone, and particularly not with Dad.

On the flip side, we took awesome family vacations around the world. Our vacations, whether near or far, were unquestionably the best part of our childhood. We often camped and hiked throughout British Columbia and traveled to Hawaii, Disneyland, Fiji, and Europe. Somehow it seemed that when we were on vacation, my parents could get along wonderfully–I am not sure why–but I suspect it was because they both valued time away so much.

In day-to-day life, to be with either Mom or Dad alone was great; it was only when we were with both that sparks flew and we learned to clear the deck. Gratefully, nevertheless, my parents' abdication from traditional parental roles opened the doors to many other and equally blessed opportunities. Self-reliance, heightened intuitive and psychic abilities, unshakable faith, and perseverance are among the greatest of my childhood blessings. Not to be overlooked is also the support received from friends, neighbors, schoolteachers, and heavenly guides and teachers who all simultaneously filled parental roles whenever necessary. There was really nothing missing in my childhood; there was just a lot of transformation.

LIFE'S MAZES

The third dance step, and one that would prove instrumental in subsequent dances, occurred in 1973. This dance step would prove to be crucial throughout the rest of my life–it was all about learning about the power of lies. Dad left our lives shortly following our fifth move in four years, a bankruptcy, and an exhausting and enlightening twelve years of volatile fights between my parents.

I still remember the day he left, as he peered inside the kitchen window asking if we would please, please unlock the door and let him in. We couldn't, because Mom swore that if we let him in, he would kill us all. By then, we really didn't know whom we were to believe. We were certainly afraid of him, but could no longer differentiate between what was real and what Mom had programmed into our heads about him. We knew he had guns, and we had seen our parents point these guns at each other, but whether he would actually pull the trigger was impossible for us to know. So we did nothing. Instead, we watched helplessly, feeling full of guilt, as he pleaded with us to let him in. In my heart, I knew this was the last time we would see him for a very long time. At the time of this last goodbye, I was seven; my little brother was six, and my older brother ten. From here on in, it would just be the four of us—my mother, my brothers, and I—or so we thought.

The next seven years would offer me some of the most revealing dance steps I was ever to learn. They involved lies, manipulation, deceit, and silence; I would come to see that all traits are powers in and of their own right—and that all propagate love. "By *Necessity*," for the course I was on, I would learn about the power of choice. In a seven-year period, I would either choose to dance or withdraw from the dance altogether, because Mom's depressed state often prompted her to suggest that we would all be better off dying and going to Heaven. I frequently found myself negotiating with her, explaining that, no matter how difficult life got, it was still worth living. In looking back, it seems that I was destined to dance no matter how hard the next step was to learn, so dance I did.

From my soul's perspective, I had scripted myself to learn what love really meant, what love really does, and, most important of all, what love overlooks. To this day, those lessons continue.

Because my mother was consumed by the belief that she was always in danger, she taught us to constantly fear for our lives. She regularly reminded us of memories of Dad's violent temper and continued rage towards her. Stories of how he was continuing to try to kill us were unending, even though we never saw him. In my heart of hearts, I knew we were safe; I knew he had gone to begin a new life without us.

For Mom, the belief of his return became paralyzing; it began to run our life. We were kept out of the school system, terrified to make friends, and lived in hiding for years to come. In the extreme times, Mom would have us change residences as often as three times in a single month, because she thought *he* was "getting closer." In addition to the moves, she changed our surname several times, just to be certain that he wouldn't be able to find us.

I intuitively knew that Mom was mentally ill and that I was often the only sane and stable force she had, so I began to mother her from that time forward. Six months after Dad's disappearance, Mom surrendered the interim custody and care of my youngest brother to Child Welfare in Abbotsford, British Columbia. Feeling overwhelmed by his hyperactive nature, she had called to see what could be done. Her feelings of rage towards his behavior were terrifying her. A social worker took the case and assigned a foster home to temporarily take him in. Mom said and believed that it would be a temporary arrangement—just until she could feel stronger in being able to handle him. Mom said her anger was coming from not being able to handle his disobedience and hyperactivity. At times, it seemed as though she hated him. I protected him as much as I could; yet I could tell that he reminded her of Dad.

My little brother was brilliant, but emotionally starved and, therefore, he searched for love and attention in the most destructive of ways. He seemed to gravitate towards anything that was very expensive or dangerous and then found a way to take it apart and analyze it. Once he broke open a car battery, which ate a large hole into the concrete floor of our garage. Another time, he broke a precious antique vase. But my most vivid memory is of the time when he accidentally broke a huge wall mirror, and Mom swore that this incident had sentenced us to suffering for the next seven years. My brother loved playing with matches, too, and Mom often wondered how "all the little fires were being put out" instead of burning the house down. I believe that we had a lot of angels working overtime.

On yet another occasion, my brother took apart Mom's favorite antique clock. Most often, however, he unconsciously tore apart the house without any awareness of the ramifications to follow. Mom never seemed to like him as much as she liked me, and she made this quite obvious, so naturally he desperately craved her attention—and tried to get it any way he could. Truly, Mom was ill equipped psychologically to handle this emotionally starved boy genius. He was seven when she dropped him off.

Three years passed—they were filled with rotations of drama. Constant changes in Mom's love affairs, business ventures, and residences were coupled with revolving jobs secured and then lost once employers discovered that she had lied about her qualifications. A cyclical pattern of wealth followed by poverty was her pattern of choice. Eventually, the cycle was broken with yet another bankruptcy induced by the legal bills incurred to try to get my brother back from Child Welfare. Mom's overwhelming feelings of desperation eventually even made her attempt to embezzle funds from financial institutions she had borrowed money from. In Mom's mind, however, all was fair in love and war–and in stealing money.

Endless talks on how to get my brother back, and countless pleas to social services to return her son, were the day-to-day conversations Mom and I engaged in. Finally, after three years, Mom was so consumed with guilt and shame for giving him up–if only temporarily–that we needed to arrange the outrageous. We decided that we would "kidnap" him from Social Services' custody, but we would need to figure out how to do this.

After exhaustive measures, we finally located the family my brother had been placed with. It was the end of the school year, and he was about to be moved again soon. If we were to snatch him, we would have to work fast. We spied on the family to see the routine my brother lived in. Next, we set the date to snatch him a couple of weeks down the road. Just days before the end of the school year, we would execute the plan. Then, weeks of organization fell apart on the day we were going to grab him because he had fallen ill and didn't go to school that day. We had planned to grab him right after the bus let him off outside his temporary home.

There was a long driveway that he had to walk up, and by the time the other children would share what had happened, we would be long gone. All the details were set, but when we saw that he was not on the bus that day, we felt dazed in disbelief that our opportunity was forever lost. Mom plunged back into depression, while I continued to pray for a miracle.

From the time I was eight until I was thirteen, we would be running and hiding either from my father or from the child protection authorities. I learned a lot about lying and becoming inconspicuous, and had become keenly sensitive to my surroundings. My life was anything but boring, and I was growing up much faster than most. My childhood playtimes happened in my virtual world–the one filled with magic, miracles, fairies, angels, and elves.

My main objective and driving force were to take care of Mom, while my older brother coped with the dramatic life changes and loss of our little brother by escaping into the world of television. He watched endless hours of comedy sitcoms and movies to blank out the insanity of Mom's actions and emotional outbursts. I coped by conversing with the nonphysical dimension and was often entertained by angels who guided me in strategies in keeping Mom from committing suicide.

Because soon after Dad left, we had little consistency in homes, money, or belongings, we learned that what was constant came from within our hearts and minds. Consequently, I learned to invest and trust in the nonphysical world instead of the external world. Most of all, from my upbringing, I learned to implicitly trust and navigate through life with my intuition, experienced as my "little voice."

From my childhood experiences, for which, as I mentioned earlier, I am deeply grateful, intuitive guidance and psychic abilities became ordinary mechanisms for psychological, physical, and emotional survival. I believe that these sixth-sense skills would not be as highly developed in me if my life had been traditional.

It is true that the more the external world dissolved, the more the internal world evolved. I was becoming a spiritual mystic without even knowing it. Seeking the instruction of my inner voice and being repeatedly touched by miracles, which are simply the expressions of love ever present, assured me that, no matter how hard life seemed to be, there was always an equalizing event occurring somewhere; I just needed to find it. And someday I would.

On a lighter note, I remember once wanting the affections of a boy so badly that I decided to play a game with him. I was ten; he was twelve, and he had big brown eyes and chocolatebrown hair. He was fascinated by magic tricks—that much I already knew—so I decided that if I wanted to get his affection, I needed to show him how magical I was. I was certain that he would be so impressed by the trick I would show him that he would be impressed with me, too!

I decided that I would tell him with 100 percent accuracy whether the coin he was holding would be heads or tails when flipped. So I proved it! He was so amazed by the trick that he seemed to overlook me. Quite obviously an entrepreneur, he thought that he could get money from his friends just by showing them my "trick." I was so upset with his remark that I vowed never to play that game again, and I didn't.

Reflections on the Dance

Looking back and viewing my life symbolically, I see the divine order. What appeared by "half-sightedness" to be missing wasn't missing at all; it did exist, but not in conventional form. I have long since realized that it was by the command of Necessity that my earthly parents needed to surrender their traditional roles, so that my heavenly parents, guides, and teachers could, in turn, have theirs. So, you might ask, would I change my childhood if I could? Not a chance!

CHAPTER 3

Dancing with Spirits, Witches, and Spells

Fantasy or Spell?

In 1973, I would learn a lot about the world of spirit. Mom was a seeker, and over the next twelve years, she would delve into every spiritual organization she stumbled upon. The first was *The Spiritualist Church of Vancouver.* On our very first visit, Mom decided that we should test the medium to see just how good she was.

We went to the flower shop and purchased a bouquet of red roses. Mom said they were actually for her deceased mother, but we would say they were for the medium who would be reading that night. We walked into the tiny church and sat in a pew at the back. About twenty minutes later, we began the service by singing my favorite hymn, *In the Garden*. It's my favorite because of the chorus line, to which I could so easily relate: "And He walks with me, and He talks with me, and He tells me I am His own..." Then we sat, and the medium began to read. I could feel the waves of coolness all around me, and somehow I just knew she was good. I did not see the spirits, although I could sense them and feel them all around. The service was just about to end when the medium walked over to the bouquet of roses and picked them up and said, "Your mother says thank you for the beautiful flowers, but next time be honest about who you are giving them to." Then she asked the person to stand and reveal who they were. Mom stood with tears rolling down her face, and the medium told her all about my grandmother and that she was okay and often with us. Then, quite by surprise, she turned to me and said, "You are a very old soul, and you have a tough, yet magical life ahead of you. You are strong and well guided, however, and I think you know that you have heaven's help, don't you?" I nodded yes. "You are actually raising her," she said, as she looked up and pointed me towards Mom's tear-filled eyes. "You would never make it without this little one," she told Mom. Then she said to me, "You will someday read for people, just like me, because you can see the world of spirit, can't you?" I nodded yes, because I had, in fact, seen spirits many times in our house, as well as angels. "You take good care of your mother because without you, she would be lost." I nodded again, and then we left the church, flowers in hand.

One of the reasons why Mom had such a pressing need to understand the spirit world was the presence of ghosts in a house we had lived in years earlier, during the time that my father was still with us. This house had been built on an ancient native burial site. So all of us children got used to sharing the house with ghosts. Doors would open and close, things would be pushed off the table, and you could hear spirits walking down the halls and stairs. Our friends and my parents' guests hated to spend the night there, but we just got used to it—after all, these ghosts never tried to harm anyone, they were just going about their business, apparently living in another dimension and completely unaware that their physical bodies were now gone. (It might be of interest here to mention that ghosts and spirit haunt-ings are not the direct actions of those who have passed on. Rather, they are remnants of emotional trauma that has not been "owned" and assimilated by those who have moved on into the spirit world. If these spirits are ultimately invited to claim the emotional experiences that they had previously disowned, such remnants of emotional trauma are assimi-lated, and the hauntings often cease.)

The next organization Mom and I became involved in was the *Rosicrucian Order*. Every Tuesday night, Mom and I would go and meditate and do spiritual healings in the temple. I loved being there, and I wanted so much to be thirteen, so that I could be the "incense girl." I envied each girl who had reached that age and was therefore permitted to sanctify the temple and light the candles before each service. There was a divine secrecy about this order that I loved. I felt as though the temple was a sacred place of worship, reverence, and healing. I knew I was privileged to be there and was expected to keep quiet about the healing and the meditations we did.

It was through this organization that Mom met Jeannette, who said that she was also a witch who practiced magic. Her next "student" would be Mom and, in some strange way, I would become her student, too. Mom and Jeannette became fast friends, and soon we were living with Jeannette and her family in order to hide from Dad. Mom and I shared a bedroom in Jeannette's home. Mom and Jeannette often talked late into the night, assuming that I was asleep—but I was not. From their discussions, I learned about some very scary and disturbing things that dwell in the minds of humans.

Jeannette had lots of books on the occult with pictures of satanic-looking creatures. The one picture I remember more than any other looked like it was half man and half animal. It had a tail; in fact, it was probably a fairly accurate depiction of what people imagine a satanic being to look like. This creature was one of Jeannette's favorite ones—in fact, she said she could communicate with it and, believe it or not, she said she regularly had sex with it, too.

Mom and Jeannette played around and put all sorts of spells on people they wanted to get even with or hurt. One day, they made potato people in the image of people they disliked, with real hair and strange "herbs," and then hacked them up into tiny pieces. Worst of all, they built a miniature replica of these people's house out of Popsicle sticks and then did a ritual and burned it. Days later, I heard Jeannette and Mom talking about how these people had had a small fire in their kitchen. They revelled in their success, while I continued to pray for these people's safety.

In retrospect, I believe that it was necessary for both the light and the dark side of spirituality to flow through my young life in order for me to decide which path I wanted to travel. Somehow I knew that I was destined for one of them and that the choice was mine to make. I never ever entertained pursuing the dark side; in fact, on a gut level, I knew that I was meant to be the counterbalance to the choice Mom had made. I think that because I had already been so protected, nurtured, and loved by heavenly beings, in many ways, the choice had been all but made. It is important to mention, however, that I believe both sides are necessary, and also come as a pair. Both can birth light and dark, and neither is better or worse, because both have the potential to propagate the idea of specialness, which translates into separation from love. I have come to understand that they are both upholding different aspects and order in and for the "Grand Orchestrating Design," or GOD.

I inherently understood energy vibrations and that "like attracts like"—that what we think about becomes our experience, and so we attract it. I knew that all things vibrated at differing speeds and that from the lowest and slowest to the highest and fastest thought, all ideas were still encompassed in the totality of love. Somehow I knew my job was to keep my vibrations high, so that the lower-thought vibrations within me could not override my powerful imagination. In moments when I began to paralyze myself in fear, I noticed that I would then attract to me all idea images and forms that vibrated in that field.

Fear stems from the belief that we have or can be separated from our Source. It is the belief that we can actually experience more pain than pleasure, or separate the pairs of opposites that make up the physical universe.

Essentially, I knew or remembered that I needed to stay balanced and appreciative of both sides. I think that the dark side is really an outpicturing of our individual and collective "shadow self"—a self that we are often terrified of, as it represents the side of ourselves that we think can usurp our Creator. The shadow self consists of the judged-against, disowned parts of our being and psyche. Stated simply, it is the part we are afraid to get to know and find nearly impossible to understand and love.

The human mind is extremely powerful, and this is true whether we use our imagination to see light in the forms of flowers and angels or through the absence thereof. In the absence of the awareness of love's pervading presence, we see the forms of demons and half-man-half-human entities.

Both sides are necessary to fully understand life, love, and our truest nature. Either way, we are interacting with our own thoughts projected outward. The dark and light are neutral in reality; it is our belief that one is better and that only one is present without the other that causes our projected fear and guilt. Remember that our perception becomes our reality, so what we think will become our experience, but not necessarily because it is true—it's just true for us. Even as a young child, I knew, or rather remembered, this.

Think about when you have a dream or nightmare, and realize that during that time, you do believe that your experience is real. It isn't—you only think it is. What your mind has done is to allow you to make pictures from your thoughts and fears. You will have peopled the parts of your psyche you both love and own, and those you fear and disown. The events in the dream will represent your beliefs, regardless of whether or not they are true.

Spells can sometimes take the form of love; spells are not love, however, because while we are under their influence, we lose our ability to see truly. Spells are half-truths. Infatuation is a spell and so is repulsion. Conversely, when we are truly in a state of love—meaning we see and appreciate both sides—we can reason more authentically than at any other time.

OLIVER TWIST

It was December of 1976, and Mom, my brother, and I lived in a tiny upstairs apartment just off Georgia Street in the city of Vancouver. Christmases had been particularly hard since Dad had left our lives, and this Christmas would be the worst—and the best. While many children wished and prayed for toys and bicycles, I wished for a turkey dinner, and for my little brother to come home.

If you consider the movie *Oliver Twist*, I was Oliver and Mom was the Master.

We would go into the major department stores and steel anything Mom fancied that day. I was to keep an eye on the sales people, while she did the "switch." If Mom wanted a new purse, wallet, fur coat, jewellery, or anything else she could "lift," I was the decoy to help her get it. In her mind, taking things she wanted wasn't really stealing, it was exchanging. She would walk in with the old item—sometimes the item that she had stolen the week before—and switch it for the new and better one! Anything she needed in order to look whatever part she was currently living in her mind was sought after. Sometimes she thought she was a royal, while other times she was a mystic, housekeeper to the Queen, or a persecuted Jew. Any painful memory that she could conjure up was created to justify in her mind that she was entitled to anything, because she had suffered so much.

Mom taught me that at Christmas time, people often felt more generous, and that we could benefit greatly from their generosity and even their guilt. She indicated to me that the churches would be giving away food and that we could be the beneficiaries if only someone would call anonymously and tell them about our situation. I loved the idea and again appreciated Mom's brilliance, but wondered who would make such a call, since we no longer had friends. By then, even the relationship with Jeannette had ended. Then, suddenly, it occurred to me that I could make the call, and so I did.

I called several churches and gave an elaborate story of a family in need. I spoke about the absolute need for an anonymous drop-off, due to the fear the family faced, since they were hiding. "Just leave the hamper on the rear deck," I urged. "Then, when the family feels safe, they will take in the hamper." I called seven churches and they all complied—all except one. One church with its grace-filled members decided they wanted to do more than just feed this family in hiding; they wanted to help further. They were the congregation members of the Vancouver Mennonite Brethren Church, and they would change our lives forever.

Three church members arrived with four heaping hampers of food, including the turkey I had secretly prayed for. They knocked at the door and waited. Ten minutes later, they knocked again, then again and again, until thirty minutes or more had passed. Finally Mom said, "Go and unlock the door and let them in, but act very surprised by yet another food delivery." By then, our tiny and normally barren kitchen was swollen with food.

The rest of that evening and the following day were all about telling the story of our recent past. Mom shared the story of the culminating events that had led up to the surrender of my brother to social services. The story had been changed to become a near-abduction of my brother by my dangerous father. My mother told this story very convincingly. The church members were sold on this heartbreaking story. Their hearts poured forth with compassion and a burning desire to help set things right.

By the middle of the following week, we were again enacting the abduction of my little brother as he left the school bus on the last day of school before the Christmas break. This time, we were successful. The children of the foster family my brother lived with didn't know what was going on. We stopped behind the bus, and then Fred, a church member, ran up to my little brother, snatched him up, and tossed him in the car. With hearts racing, we drove off and the car slid into a fence, but the driver, another church member, regained control and fled away. Stricken with fear of being captured, we were fleeing yet again.

One of the church members decided that we needed to get out of the province of British Columbia, and so he took us to Winnipeg, and then to Morden to the house of his mother and father. Within one month, he had fallen under Mom's captivating spell, and soon thereafter, he announced their engagement. Three months later, they were married and pregnant. My brothers and I were settling into our newly extended family. My stepdad was 28, hardworking, a devout Christian, and so naïve when he met us. He had no idea what he was getting into–and neither did my brothers and I.

I had seen so many men before fall for Mom's fantastic lies and intoxicating kiss. She was a beauty, and I watched silently, while knowing in my heart that Mom was like the black widow spider, waiting for the perfect time to kill, in order for her lies and demons to survive. She wasn't trying to be cruel as much as she was surviving. All of her deluded stories about the past were a by-product of who she perceived she was and the experiences she had had. The bitterness she perceived her life to have been filled with was in her mind a license to do whatever it took to get back at anyone and everyone. Therefore, it was only a matter of when–not if–she would destroy this mate, too.

Ron, my step-dad, had grown up a Mennonite in Morden, Manitoba. He was one of 13 children and, by his account, had been raised by a strong, disciplinary hand. Ron was normally self-controlled and very kind, but even he would be pushed to his limits in a relationship with Mom.

We set up house in the city of Winnipeg following a brief four-month stint in the town of Kalida, our first house of hiding. Then, the following spring, the entire family was baptized Mormon. Months earlier, we had been visited by Elders of the Church in Winnipeg. Mom had done her homework and discovered that the Mormon

Church was well structured and wealthy enough to set up an internal financial assistance program for the less fortunate "brothers and sisters" of the Church. Knowing our heart-wrenching story, and seeing that we needed extended financial support, yet another plan was devised. The Bishop in Winnipeg agreed with Mom's logic that more help was needed, and it was decided that we should move to an area where there would be a much bigger support network of brothers and sisters. The Bishop urged us to move to Southern Alberta, where there were more resources and "family" to care for us.

In May 1978, my half-brother was born in Lethbridge, Alberta. Many, including Church members and family, blessed his homecoming. We lived off Church resources until my parents could get back onto their feet. Six months later, they left the Church. Mom said, "The Mormons down here are hypocrites, not at all like Winnipeg Mormons." Once again, she felt justified in her mind that we had been betrayed and therefore had the right to abandon the fold; from her point of view, no repayment of kindness was necessary.

Reflections on the Dance

Having had such a rich and diversified life, I learned that, in reality, there was no right or wrong. There were only differing perceptions that gave rise to differing values and priorities. By age fourteen, I had attracted life circumstances that had afforded me the opportunity to learn this.

CHAPTER 4

*L*earning to *D*ance or *D*ie

By age sixteen, I had had enough of living in what felt like captivity to me. I was "timed" almost everywhere I went, to ensure that I had not stopped to talk to the boys, or to anyone else. Mom knew exactly how long it took to get home from school, and every minute over the time limit had a price tag attached to it. Often the price came in the form of yelling, and sometimes in the form of a beating, both physically and emotionally. Many of my actions were overly scrutinized, and I was frequently accused of lying—even though I was telling the truth. Between my parents and myself, trust was missing, and feelings of suffocation were building.

Ever since Mom had met and married Ron, my stepdad, she had changed. She would tell Ron that we had been disobedient and disrespectful while he was at work. She was great at putting on quite a show, a natural actress, which I am, too. She could get Ron so riled that he would lose reasoning faculties and would beat us black and blue, or physically push us around the house until we were ready to "be good." Naturally, I began to compare my life to the way my friends lived, which seemed to magnify the feelings of "injustice" and unfair treatment that I had never recognized before, because we had never stayed anywhere long enough to make friends.

What I later figured out through reflection on my childhood was that Mom was terrified that I would tell Ron the truth of her colorful past. The fact that he was a highly moral chap and Mom was the opposite had created quite a problem in her mind. Therefore, she had to minimize my character and integrity in order to be certain that, should I speak up, my stories of years previous would be seen as unreliable. Mom's top concern was keeping her past hidden. Her reputation of innocence was highest on her list of values to protect, and so all else would be sacrificed. Realize that no one is really committed to anyone else; they are truthfully only committed to their values. Mom's value was to look good in Ron's eyes, and so she needed to devalue me, in case I decided to tell the truth.

One of Mom's deepest secrets that I held in my heart, as I once held all her secrets, was that Mom had become pregnant by a fellow she was dating. The fellow turned out not to be what she had expected, and she decided not to keep the baby—she aborted the pregnancy. I just knew it had been a boy—the name that came to my mind was Andrew. In order to appease her guilt over the abortion, and so as not to have to explain her actions, she made up the story that she had been raped.

Guilt that an individual perceives will be projected onto another. This, in turn, will give rise to the perception of whatever we feel guilty about, by the other. Thus, I was regularly accused of being untruthful, manipulative, and too fixated on boys. All those things were true, of course, but not exactly in the ways Mom was implying. I wanted to feel loved and approved of, as most teens do. I desperately sought the approval of others, and would do anything I could to feel wanted. I wanted to do sleepovers with girlfriends and hang out with "the gang." I wanted to feel normal, and to be a kid. Because I was not openly allowed to do so, I snuck out at night, missed the bus purposely, or did anything else that would allow me to get what I felt was important, or missing from my life—in other words, to get my values met. All my desires went against Mom's values, so we found it hard to communicate; we had a careless/careful relationship, which means there was an imbalance in recognizing the equal importance of our differing values.

Since Mom had unexpectedly become pregnant more than once, had had multiple sex partners, and lied as easily as she told the truth, she perceived I would do the same. Because she never stopped to consider the other side or "blessings" that came out of those hidden and shame-filled actions, she was being psychologically and behaviorally motivated by half-truths, which are distortions of perception. Since these distortions were the filters through which she saw me, accusations of my dishonesty were predictable and unavoidable until she learned to love those parts of herself. Half the truth of her being was all she was facing; therefore, half my being was all she could see.

Her culminated fears about promiscuity were then projected onto me, which also meant that one day, her fear would be realized. It would be realized because one of the universal principles is that we will eventually attract what we do not love. I refer to this universal law as the CAB© Principle: *Anything you do not love, you will Create, Attract, or Become.*

I should mention that there are well over 4,500 human traits, and that we all have them in some area of our life, either expressed or repressed. In fact, the situations and people we attract are designed to help us discover, uncover, and then recover from the illusion that we only want positive traits. Since love encompasses two sides—the negative and the positive—we are destined to recognize that love is never missing from our life. Remember love is the complement of all traits, so we are here on earth to learn how to find both sides, which, when seen, reveal love's constant presence. Consequently, all the traits we have that we arbitrarily divided into good and bad must then be recognized as necessary aspects of the whole and holy self.

Because my home life felt so confining and limiting, I wanted out. In retrospect, I see that the flip side of the confinement I felt was that I was allowed to have my own job, my own car, and I was driving long before I had a driver's license. In that area of my life, my parents trusted me fully. Like many teens, however, I felt overly controlled and confined, and therefore inevitably tried to find a way to break out of my parents' constraints. For years, I pleaded to do just that. I begged to be given up to a foster home, or to be released into the care of Social Services. I even asked if I could go live with my parents' friends. All my requests were denied. Yet, I felt as though I could not endure one more day at home, where I felt unwanted and disowned, so I devised a plan. In my mind, there was only one way out, and one place where I knew I was cared for and wanted: that place was heaven, and my way out was death.

The deep sense of sorrow, abandonment, and inadequacy I felt was inevitable, given that I had begun to see only one side of my life experiences. The *neutral* archetype of *Victim* or *Victor* remained in my life. However, depending upon whether I was able to see both sides of any situation, I began polarizing my perception into one side or the other. My limited sight and lack of questioning of what were the benefits of the challenges I was confronting was, in turn, beginning to show me *Victim's* other face. In my earlier years, I just knew that everything had two sides, and that they were both necessary in order to grow in love and wisdom. All throughout my life, this archetype showed up as it does in all people's lives, yet in previous years, I had spontaneously chosen the side of *Victor* rather than *Victim*.

I suppose that, since Mom had been playing *Victim*, and we never receive only one side of a particular trait or archetype, I needed to play out the other side. After her marriage to Ron, she began feeling more victorious, and I automatically became the counterbalance, meaning that I now played the role of *Victim*. Remember that opposites, which I have referred to as the two sides of the magnet, are inseparable. Each of us, then, was playing one half of the two-sided archetype. I was equilibrating *Victor* by playing out the side of *Victim*.

Over time, I had slowly fallen asleep to the *Victim* side and begun playing out the equal and opposite side of the

Victim—the *Victor*. In other words, I had stopped considering the many strengths, blessings, and gifts that had been cultivated as a result of my perfect childhood. I had contracted my life plan to learn the deeper meaning of love—to live through both sides of all situations and traits, in order to experience the real meaning of love. Therefore, like my parents, until I saw two sides, I was viewing my life through a perception half-seen.

DESPAIR AND DEATH

I had fallen hard for a guy named Stephen, whom I had met while working at the Dairy Queen. He was from Prince George, and in my mind, he was possibly my way out of my parents' house, or so I prayed. After a week of dating, we decided that I would go back to his hometown with him. My hopes were crushed, however, when a friend told me that Stephen already had a girl back home. The realization that Stephen was not going to take me anywhere hit me hard right in the solar plexus and the heart—he was going home to "her," and my hoped-for chance to leave home evaporated; I plummeted into despair.

The following Monday afternoon, my parents had some friends over to our house, and I was told to keep an eye on their children, while the adults were busy chatting. I was thinking about death as a way out of my hopelessness. I had thought about dying many times before, and it did not frighten me at all. I knew that "I" wouldn't die; I would just get rid of my body, and finally get out of the house I perceived to be hell.

I began methodically taking small quantities of many

different pills, ranging from anti-inflammatory drugs to painkillers, that Mom had gathered over the previous ten years. Some of these pills were for dogs and some for humans; some had an expiration date that had long passed. I timed my ingestion–I needed to, if I was to do it right. Every 20 minutes, a few more pills. Then I walked into the living room and stared at the gorgeously framed picture of Jesus that hung on the wall. It was so surreal. He stared back at me, not a word spoken. This was not like times before, when we would converse on how to help and support others. This time it was I that felt broken, irreparable, and so, so sad. Suddenly, rage surfaced, and I said in disbelief, "You promised me that you wouldn't give me more than I could handle...you lied. I'm done here, I'm coming home, and not even you can stop me."

Moments turned into hours–everyone home, yet too busy to notice what was happening with me. No one was present enough to see my glazed-over eyes, my shattered heart, or my desperate act. I was becoming disoriented. I made a final call to my friends at work–to say goodbye and to tell them that Stephen had betrayed me and that he had another girl back home. I hung up the phone, stepped into the bathroom, closed the door, and dropped to the floor, unconscious. The friends whom I had called realized that something was wrong with me, and called back. My parents answered the phone, which hung on the wall opposing the bathroom. When they learned that I had made that desperate call to my friends, they came looking for me.

The next things I remember are streetlights, Ron's face filled with fear and screaming, "Wake up!" Then there was blackness...then doors rushing open...more bright lights, then blackness...then having my stomach pumped...then blackness again. Then the pain stopped and unspeakable peace and love filled my being. Suddenly, I was hovering over my limp body; I saw crash carts, sorrow, and my friends in tears. I was floating through the hospital, into the waiting room, then back into the emergency room. It was eerie–I seemed to be in many places all at once; with every thought came an instantly different experience. If I thought "Mom," there she was, but simultaneously I was wherever someone else thought of me, too. It felt like I was everywhere and nowhere. I was much more expansive than I had ever imagined, or remembered. Frantically, they worked on me, and then, suddenly, I was filled with light and back "in the Garden" with Jesus, where I had spent much time in my younger years, although it seemed to be in my mind rather than an actual place.

"You have to go back," He said.

"No, I won't, I can't, it's too hard...it's too painful," I answered.

"You have not finished your life there yet, you have much more to do...children to have, and people to help," said Jesus.

"I can't live there, it is too hard; I won't go back. Please, don't make me," I pleaded.

"What if you didn't have to stay with them [my parents] anymore? What if you could move out?" He said.

"Then I would go back, but you have to promise that I can leave right away."

"I promise," He said.

Then, with a jolt, I was back in my body. It felt horrible, tight, and so confining–then I fell asleep.

I was later told that I had been clinically dead for 17 minutes while the doctors and nurses worked unceasingly to bring me back to life. Five days passed as I lay in a coma. Then on the fifth day, I awoke. I told the nurse what had happened to me, what I had seen, and where I had gone. She was dumbstruck as I told her in detail what I had seen—the crash carts, the defibrillator, the waiting room. I asked about my friends, and I wanted to know where my parents were. She said they all called to check in daily; she would call them to come. "No, not yet," I said. I fell asleep.

Next, I underwent psychological evaluations. This was the standard procedure for patients who had attempted suicide. I knew that if I told the doctor about the abuse that I perceived in my childhood, he would be horrified and investigate. I lied and told only a part of the real story—the part about my boyfriend having another girlfriend. I told him I knew it was silly to take it all so seriously. I faked my way through all his questions brilliantly—I was my mother's daughter; I knew how to lie, better than most.

MY TICKET TO FREEDOM

My ticket to freedom came through our Japanese neighbor's son, Al. I will call him dance partner number seven. My brothers were number three and four, and my first puppy love, Scott Masters, was number five. The "Magician" was number six. Dance partner seven, like all my previous dance partners, would do just one dance before he would leave.

The day after my psychological evaluation, Al, who was 21, came to see me in the hospital. I think he intuitively knew what was going on at our house, and he probably suspected that leaving home was my next move. He wanted to move out, too, but needed a roommate. I knew that he had a crush on me, and that he would like to have me for his girlfriend. I also realized that he was what I needed to be able to escape, so I compromised what I really felt about him—I lied. During Al's half-day visit, we developed a verbal "contract," although I never told him my plan, or the way I was going to use him. I would begin by moving in with him, but sleep in my own bed. Then, after a while, we would see if the friendship could be cultivated into a romantic relationship. Enter in the archetypal pattern of the *Prostitute*. We may find it difficult to admit, but we all prostitute in some areas of our life. Take an honest look at yourself, and you will see where you are willing to "sell out" for your physical, financial, emotional, or spiritual survival. For example, I know that, throughout my life, there were moments when I wanted to leave a love relationship, but was afraid for my own financial well-being and thus chose to stay instead.

After I was released from the hospital, Al and I moved into an apartment together. However, two weeks later, I moved out, because I realized that he had a private agenda: to have sex with me. His sexual tensions and "comeons" were more than I could bear. I had used Al to get out of my parents' house, which, at that time, had been my highest value. I left his place with mixed emotions, having nowhere to go, but finally feeling free. During the following weeks, I slept in and lived out of my car.

The archetype of the *Prostitute*, like the *Victim*, is neutral in and of itself; it is polarized only when we let fear or guilt govern our decision in moving forward. For instance, I might have the desire to get financially ahead when an opportunity to do so comes along. The only thing I need to decide is if the opportunity is congruent with my current morals and values. If it is not, the archetype questions us to see if morals or secure outcomes are more important at this time. The *Prostitute* archetype is there to help us decide whether we will negotiate our spirit or integrity to get what we want now.

These archetypal patterns of influence are not attached to which choice we make as much as they are attached to seeing what currently drives our decisions, fears, guilt, or love. All archetypes are parts of our psychological make-up. These "parts" have formed (and are still forming) from a culmination of traits and qualities that have evolved, both individually and collectively, over millennia. Specific traits and qualities, when woven together, create a filter through which we make our daily decisions.

You have all the willpower in the world to break any habit.
The power of divine will is always with you,
and can never be destroyed.

Paramahansa Yogananda

CHAPTER 5

When Despair Dances with Miracles

One evening in early autumn, I was cruising the strip in Lethbridge. The previous two months had been a combination of true gypsy life—bouncing between my car, friends' homes, and rented rooms. That night, I parked my car at the local hangout for teens. This is where I met my next dance partner, Marc, who would be the biological father of my first daughter. The year was 1980. I was a virgin, 16, and going on 20. He was 19, not a virgin, and in my eyes gorgeous. He had a gentle spirit, big blue eyes, blond Afro-styled hair, and a great body. He was a car buff. We hung out and fooled around for three weeks before we had sex.

It was Halloween night—Oct 31; 22 days after my 16th birthday. This evening would prove to be magical and life-altering in some unforeseen way. I wanted desperately to be loved by someone, so much so that this was the day that I turned in my virginity. That night, in the explosion of passion, my daughter Emma was conceived. Within minutes of our sexual interlude, I could feel that something profound and marvellous was on its way. Emma is now 25 years old; but wait, I have leaped ahead, so let's go back in time and see how the events unfolded.

Two weeks after conceiving, I called Marc to confirm what I had known for a while in the depth of my being. I said, "I'm pregnant and we should talk." Three days later, while standing in my rented room, I said to him, "I will keep this baby, no matter what." Inside, I knew that I wanted desperately to be loved, and if not by him, then for sure it would be by this little gift—this precious soul. He stood there, fear-stricken, and dumbfounded by my certainty. "I'll tell you the choices I have to offer you," I continued. "The first is that we continue to hang out and see if in time we could live together and maybe even down the road get married. We will share the load of caring for the baby; we will take it day by day." This was the choice I desperately wanted him to take, as I was very much in love with him. Of course, I did not clue in then that what he had wanted were unlimited amounts of sex. "Choice number two is that you walk out of here and you'll have no rights to the child; I will raise the baby and you get off scot-free." He thought about it for five minutes, and then announced that he had decided on door number two. The prize was absolute freedom from financial and emotional responsibility. We hugged; he wished me good luck, and I began my dance with motherhood!

Seven weeks later, I was cruising again—still looking for love in all the wrong places. I had the sweetest little 1968 metallic emerald-green Volkswagen Karman Ghia, which was known around town as the "little green car with the pretty blonde." While waiting at a red stoplight, I looked to my right, and there he was. He—Adam—looked at me, the light turned green; he gave a half smile, and then tore off in his brand new cherry-red MJB convertible.

Destiny was hard at work, however, because as he approached the next block intersection, he encountered yet another red light. Again I pulled up beside him; again he looked over and smiled. This dance went on for three more blocks, and then Adam gave me a nod to pull over. I did, and we began to talk. Soon I realized that he was deeply wounded and troubled in every area of his life. His child-hood seemed to have been very difficult, his girlfriend had left him, and he had just lost his apartment. He had been accused of stealing from his uncle, and he hated the depart-ment he worked in at a local hotel. That night, we talked for hours; I told him I was pregnant, and that the baby's father had left me. Adam said, "What a dishonorable guy, what a loser! I would never walk away from a life I had created. "

Remember, however, what I stated earlier—that there is a fundamental law at work in the universe that ordains that *anything* or *any action* you do not love, you will *create, attract,* or *become.* And time would prove this true—even for Adam and our future children.

I can now see that we were both "lost children" our-selves, both trying to make it big in an adult world. I wanted to be *the first* to unconditionally love him. "As a woman thinketh–so shall she perceive." If only I had understood then what I know now–in that if I wanted to experience to what degree I could test love, the cosmos was willing to offer me the experience. It is the arrogance of the ego voice that says, "I am special and I can love you like no other." Of course, in reality, we had both been loved; it was we who had not loved ourselves unconditionally, and so we projected the illusion of a "missing or conditioned love" onto the world. Further, it would be safe to say we were still spellbound by a fantasized and unrealistic view of romantic love that no one can attain.

This is a good time to remind that love, like light, is the synthesis of two opposite sides coming together in perfect balance–the love coin that has two sides. Each trait is connected with its opposite–cruel with kind, stingy with generous, life with death, the seen with the unseen, hot with cold, and dark with light. In life and in light, positively and negatively charged particles surround us in perfect balance, but if we cannot see that both the negative and positive are present, we will feel as though something is missing, and we will begin feeling pulled in one direction. We will be viewing people and situations with one eye closed.

Because the law and order of the universe is equilibrium, something must show up to balance us out, if we do not balance ourselves out. So when Adam perceived that his parents were too strict, the right question to ask was: Where was there too much leniency? I can tell you the answer: it was in him. Much of that was true in my own childhood as well. Both of us had a long journey ahead in learning about the power of a disciplined will. The will identifies the power of our thoughts and actions. We actually do experience what we think about and what we have not learned to love.

Since we both had fantasized and romanticized notions of what love was, we both thought that to be loved meant that all was good, easy, hot, and steamy. Because we can't have just one side, perceived pain was inevitable.

If you have been in any relationship, you will have discovered that it is both good and bad—that is why it is love. It is why metaphysical people say that love is all there is. Since good and bad are perceptions based on projected differing values, beliefs, and circumstances, it is whichever is perceived—the good or the bad—that will attract its opposite.

For instance, a farmer wants rain, while the sunbather wants sun; for each, no matter which is "better," the opposite will also be present and affect them in some area of life. The sunbather who got sun or, in their perception, good, needs to water the lawn. Similarly, the farmer who got rain needs to bring the laundry in off the clothesline.

In time, I discovered that to love Adam would also mean to meet parts of myself that I hid from, denied, and avoided. At the time of our relationship, I often felt more evolved, and therefore able to forgive him, for the many lies, half-truths, and betrayals I experienced from him.

Subsequently, I have learned that neither forgiveness nor pardon was necessary on my part. Both implied arrogance, since both stemmed from the belief that my values ought to be his also. Through the study of light and love, I have learned that we all lie when we feel our desires, values, or priorities are being threatened. Any time we feel that what we value is in danger of being lost, we will lie or do whatever it takes to secure this value. Truthfully, we are only committed to our values or to those people who help us get our values. Nevertheless, for Adam and me, our souls came together to dance a dance that would forever leave etchings of change on us both. We would learn about love, and that would undoubtedly last a lifetime.

Over the next 14 years, Adam would become one of my greatest teachers, and my greatest adversary. Of course, he would present "both sides," since that is what it takes to teach about the deepest meaning and the transformational power of love.

Within the first year of our being together, we had moved from Lethbridge to Calgary and broken up four times. From my perception, I had repeatedly been betrayed, cheated on, and lied to, all this with my baby girl in tow.

In our second year of marriage, I had become pregnant again, even though I had been taking birth control pills. When I was eight weeks pregnant, we broke up again, and Adam left. He seemed to have these love-hate feelings towards me; it was hard for me to understand his extreme emotions.

I realized years later that his anger towards me was allowed to manifest because firstly, I allowed him to be abusive—not standing up for myself; secondly, I thought that unconditional love meant that I should keep "forgiving"; thirdly, I was internally beating myself up and he was expressing that to me; and lastly, I had an uncanny ability to challenge someone's values, often unconsciously. I now realize that the guilt he often felt for the way he treated me had poisoned his emotional body, so that when he looked at me, all that past guilt rushed forward and eclipsed the present opportunity to love. Deep in my heart, I always knew that he didn't want me; he loved and yearned for his first girlfriend, and then with time, it seemed, for anyone but me.

By 1984, our relationship and my heart felt so bruised and battered that I knew we could never recover. I was 21 and pregnant with my third daughter. Adam had, once again, moved out. As my delivery day approached, I discovered that he was living with another woman. In fact, as I would find out later, while I was delivering and recovering with my new baby girl, the other woman, whom I will call Eve, was watching my two older girls. In the days following our daughter's birth, he announced to me that he had found his soulmate, and it was Eve.

It's strange how soul contracts sometimes override our reason, and our human understanding. I knew that Adam loved other women beside me, yet his soul seemed to know something our humanness didn't. His soul believed that if he was to evolve spiritually, he needed to one day come to love me. The timing would be up to him, but that he would eventually love me was destined. Whether he loves me in this or a subsequent lifetime is not the issue. The issue is to learn to love, and to love means to appreciate a person or situation "as is"–and especially those who have tested us on every level.

Through Adam's and my journey together, I learned that we are destined to dance with certain individuals, even when the music seems to have stopped. In fact, the silent dances are those that are going on even when we appear to be on different dance floors, separated by time and space. Those dances seem to be the ones that evolve our soul without our conscious awareness.

In *A Course in Miracles*, we are taught that all relationships are eternal. They are holy encounters. It reminds us that the loving and appreciating we learn to do of our perceived shadow self and that of our partner transcend understanding. I have since realized that the very thing in which it is most difficult to see the order or divinity is also that which leaps us upward and into the hands of God faster than anything else.

TRANSPORTED ON THE WINGS OF LOVE

In December 1984, my newborn daughter Sara was barely three weeks old, and I needed some support in handling the reality that my husband was going to permanently leave me for another woman. I drove to Calgary to stay with a friend and figure out how I would manage life with three young children. During the evening of my arrival there, Sara became very, very ill. I took her to Calgary Children's Hospital, where she was admitted immediately. It was discovered that she had bronchial pneumonia, and her life was in danger. They shaved her tiny head, hooked her up to an IV, and eventually to life support. The doctors weren't sure if she would survive. They advised me to inform her father in case she would not live until the morning. Now Sara and I were both fighting to survive—she physically and I emotionally.

I called Adam at the restaurant where he worked. He answered the phone, and I informed him of the seriousness of the situation. I told him that he should come to Calgary to see Sara. He reluctantly agreed, but said I would have to come and pick him up, since he had no vehicle that could make the trip. I agreed.

It's a two-hour drive between Lethbridge and Calgary; I made it in 90 minutes. It was 11:30 P.M. when I arrived at the hotel. I walked into the dining room to meet Adam. He announced that he had decided not to come with me after all. I was shocked and confused, I pleaded, he refused, and I left.

I went across the street to the gas station and called my friend in Calgary to check on my two girls, whom she was watching. I needed to let her know what had happened; I was crying and trying to sort out my thoughts and the appropriate actions. I told her that, on my way back, I would swing by my house and get some extra clothes for the girls, since I would undoubtedly be in Calgary much longer than I had originally anticipated. I told her I would stop by her house on the way back to the hospital to leave the extra clothes and then head back to the hospital. I finished the conversation stating that I did not know how long I would be at the hospital, but that I would keep her informed.

Approximately twenty minutes later, I pulled up to my home to discover Eve's car parked in front of my house. I felt confused and shattered as I searched for a reason other than what was obvious, why she would be at our home. Apparently, Adam still had a key, and since Eve had a roommate, her place did not offer them the privacy they wanted, so they had come here, thinking that I wouldn't be home.

I walked into the house; Adam and Eve were both inside, startled by my sudden entry into the living room. I was speechless as I saw a blanket, a bottle of wine, some movies, crackers, and cheese all neatly laid out on my living room floor. They were preparing for a romantic picnic...

I lost my composure and began crying, raging, and pleading for some understanding. Then, suddenly, instinctual childlike and maternal feelings flooded my body. I was like a mother bear that perceived her cubs in danger. I ran up the stairs to the kitchen, began scanning the drawers, and grabbed the largest knife I could find. I had never felt such rage; I felt disorientated, and my heart ached in disbelief. I felt completely abandoned, emotionally and physically—time stood still.

Suddenly, a wave of warmth filled my being and an inner voice said, "Put down the knife. The baby needs you, the girls need you, and this is not the answer." Defeated, I surrendered. I listened to the voice and set down the knife. I left the house, got into my car, and for the second time in my life, I told Jesus that this was too much to bear. I begged for help as I sobbed, barely able to see the road through my tears.

To this day, I have no memory of the trip that followed. The only memory I have is of the moment I suddenly found myself at a stoplight at the Southland Drive intersection on the edge of Calgary. It felt like only a moment had passed from the time I raced down the highway to get back to the hospital, to the time I sat waiting for the light to turn green. Within moments, I was rounding the corner to my girlfriend's house. I knocked softly, then again; the porch light came on, and she cracked open the door. Speechless she stood, staring at me, "How did you get here so fast?" she asked. "I drove," I replied. "That can't be—you called me about 25 minutes ago." I was too confused to get her point. All I wanted to do was to get to my baby girl before she died. I dropped off the clothing and headed downtown to see if Sara was still alive. When I arrived at the hospital, she was still in critical condition; she remained in this state for three days, after which a miraculous turnaround began.

Weeks passed, and Sara fully recovered. With her recovery came the torture of fully accepting the idea that I was going to be on my own with three little children. Although Adam and I had separated before, we had always come back together shortly after the birth of each of the first two babies. This time, I just knew things were going to be different. I was consumed by my racing mind, desperately trying to figure out a way to get Adam back. I deeply wanted our family to be back together and, in spite of all the problems and perceived abuse, I wanted to be his wife.

Adam was confused also, so he was alternately telling both Eve and me that he wanted to be with us, and was "arranging" it. For the next three weeks, he would flip-flop between beds, and then I had finally had enough. I arranged for a babysitter and drove to Eve's house, where they were living together. It was about 1 P.M. I knocked, she answered; she seemed without surprise, and wanted to talk with me.

We decided to go to the Boston Pizza down the street, where we talked for six hours. We talked about everything from my childhood to their great sex life. My motive for the talk was to see what was so "special" about her—to identify it and, if at all possible, duplicate it, so I could get Adam back.

After spending some time with her, I realized that she would probably have become a friend had we met under different circumstances. She was warm, sincere, and pretty.

In fact, I saw a lot of personality similarities between us, and I could see why Adam had fallen for her.

In spite of everything, however, I still wanted to understand why she was willing to tear apart our family. I wanted to understand why she would date a married man who was expecting a new baby. In response, she said that Adam had initially told her that his marriage was over and that there was no chance of reconciliation, and that she had believed him.

She shared with me her childhood and how her mother had died when she was 13. She told me that she had been hospitalized for psychiatric assessment in the months to follow because of her depressed and uncontrollable behavior. In addition, she shared how hard her childhood had been. She had suffered greatly because of her alcoholic father. At a young age, she had become involved in an incestuous relationship. It became obvious to me that she was troubled by her past, just as Adam and I were troubled by our respective pasts.

I wanted to let Eve know that Adam had been telling me that he couldn't get rid of her because she wouldn't let go of him—that he really loved me, and that he wanted our family back. She was stunned by my messages, because Adam was telling her exactly the same things about me. In my heart, I knew that she was telling the truth and that a very confused puppeteer was playing her and me like puppets. I told her then that I was through with Adam, and that she could have him.

Even though I had made my decision, I wanted to know why she felt that she loved him so much. This turned out to have been the wrong question to ask! Eve told me, with a glow of certainty, that Adam was "the guy"—the soulmate that she had been looking for, and she had never been so happy. She was amazed with how loving and caring Adam was—not only to her, but to his girls also. She told me how he cared for her, ironed her work clothes, tidied the house, and rubbed her back. I was stunned. He had never washed a dish in our home, not even when I had delivered our babies. No matter what, I would always come home to a sink full of dirty dishes.

Eve then dropped the final bomb on my heart by innocently mentioning that she had watched the two older girls while I was delivering Sara. How could he, I thought. He had *her* watch my girls, while I delivered our baby—how sick! "He never rubbed *my* back, ironed *my* clothes, or did any of the other things you say he does for you," I told Eve. I was confused. Were we talking about the same person?

After our discussion, we drove to Adam's place of work, where we both announced that we were done with him. I went home. A few hours later, he called me on the phone, sobbing and pleading with me to talk to Eve and convince her that he and I were, in fact, finished. He said he was certain that she was his soulmate and that he was sorry for all the pain and suffering he had put me through. He admitted that he had never felt for me what he was feeling for her. He assured me that he really loved her and couldn't bear to live without her. He pleaded with me to help save their relationship, since we were through. I thought about it, realized that my relationship with him was over, and agreed to call Eve. I called her and assured her that since he had done so much for her, he must deeply care for her. I reminded her that if he was her soulmate, she should not just cast him away. She listened; I assured her that I no longer wanted to be his wife, and they made up.

Reflections on the Dance

Upon reflection, I can see that there have been many miracles in my life, and I will share them with you throughout this book. However, what is of equal importance as the miracles themselves is the love that inspired them. The love that was there, no matter how ugly one side looked. The pleasure in this particular story came from my finally being able to end my relationship with Adam, and eventually increasing my self-esteem and regaining my personal power. It was no longer up to him to choose which one of us he wanted, since I had dropped out of the race.

I have discovered repeatedly that when we are pushed to a particular place of surrender, something not of this world emerges. That something is grace. I absolutely know that in my life the grace and love of the universe will carry me when I can no longer carry myself. If I can remember to ask and receive, with an open and willing heart, all the experiences that come that are mine to embrace, authentic power becomes mine.

DIVINE GUIDANCE

The months passed, and I struggled to keep going. The only friend I had at the time was a renounced Mormon friend who had gone metaphysical. We spent endless hours discussing the deeper meaning of life. She had a difficult marriage and often questioned what life would be like on my side of the fence, while I yearned to be on her side, which meant having a husband and jointly raising a family. It was the proverbial "grass is greener" perspective, which we often discussed—she wanted my side, I wanted hers.

One day, while I was visiting with them and their three daughters, her husband did a tarot card reading for me. It was my first tarot reading, and I had no idea if it had any validity. However, once the reading had begun, both he and I were sorry we had asked what was in store for my future. He said he saw another marriage that would produce two boys. Then, yet another divorce, followed by more time alone, and then a third marriage. He said there would be a lot of relocating and a lot of trials yet to endure. He warned me of some "private agendas" by a dark-haired woman. I assumed he meant my gypsy mother, but have since realized that it was Adam's girlfriend Eve he was picking up on. He later said, "You will marry again and have a new life." He continued by saying that I was actually living two lifetimes, but with one body. I needed to hang on no matter what, no matter how hard things would get, until I was between 30 and 35 and ready to start my second life—a life with huge impact upon humanity. A life filled with joy and opportunity.

A MOTHER'S LOVE

Five months after Sara's birth, and following an enormous struggle to regain some of my self-esteem, lost because of the infidelity in our marriage, Adam made a suggestion that forever changed the direction in which our lives went. He suggested that he and his girlfriend Eve would take the girls to live with them. I was outraged, and I refused. A week later, the same request came again, as he told me that if I really loved the girls, I would do what was best for them, not me. That comment hit me right in the gut. My withered sense of self was so crippled that I began to consider his words. It was true that I was struggling in every area in my life, emotionally, psychologically, and financially. I was working long hours at multiple jobs and could no longer find the resources to give more than I was giving, but he could, and he reminded me of that weekly. My heart and head felt torn apart, moving me in opposing directions. It reminded me of a childhood story I had heard in Sunday School of King Solomon and the two mothers. As I recalled the biblical story, King Solomon was asked to decide on who was the true mother, since they both claimed the child as their own. His decision to divide the baby in half whirled through my mind. What would love have me do?

In the biblical story, there is a dispute over the baby between the natural mother and the acting mother. Both claim to be the real mother wanting to keep the child. The opposing parties are both proclaiming a deep and unconditional love for the child. King Solomon is not sure who is telling the truth, so he suggests that he would kill the child, offering each "mother" a half.

The acting mother seems to find this decision acceptable, while the natural mother is horrified and replies that she would rather see the child raised by the acting mother than its life taken. In some strange mythological way, it seemed that I had also been given such a choice.

The division between what my mind rationalized I should do, and what my heart and soul whispered was my ultimate journey, was tearing me apart. In my heart of hearts, I knew my soul contract was to surrender my children to "a better life than I could give them," for now.

In other words, the soul contract felt larger than my human understanding of this event. In some profound way, I understood how Jesus must have felt in the Garden of Gethsemane, as He asked God if this cup could be taken away. I, like Jesus, needed to drink of this experience to evolve. So I did.

A couple of weeks later, I surrendered the girls. I wanted desperately to believe that, if the three of us worked together, it would be better for the children than what I alone could ever do for them. But while I know that it could have been a beautiful way to co-parent the girls, this was not what they had planned. Initially, I agreed to a trial period of this new arrangement and moved the girls from my place to Adam and Eve's house for the summer. Packing up my daughters' rooms was one of the hardest things I have ever done.

This event reminded me of a movie I had seen just months before, of a Jewish mother leaving for the concentration camps. Merrill Streep acted as a Jewish mother who was being sent away. In one particular scene, she was asked to choose between her daughter and her son. The soldier indicated that, through her choice, one would be freed, while the other would go with her to die. That's how I felt; death was now a lever of life, and that day, a part of me died.

The weeks following were excruciatingly painful for me. I would go and visit the children between jobs and then, as I was preparing to leave for work, the girls would cry, begging me not to leave them as they clung to my leg.

Each time I had to leave them, another piece of my heart was torn out, guilt consumed me, and in time I began to go numb. Soon I began avoiding the visits, believing they were too hard on the girls. I didn't realize, however, that Eve was feeling abandoned by me, and in time I would understand the huge impact that Eve's perception of her abandonment by me would have on the next fourteen years of my life. By the end of August, I couldn't take it anymore, and thoughts of abducting the girls raced through my mind. What prevented me from doing so was that I didn't want my children to go through the same childhood experiences that I had had. In my mind, there was no escape, and no answer.

I was working at three jobs to help make ends meet for myself and to help support the girls' physical needs. Eve was three months pregnant and unable to work, so I worked harder to provide for the kids and myself. Soon I stopped eating, and then sleeping; I was dying of heartbreak and was overwhelmed with guilt and confusion for my actions. I could no longer reason rationally, my self-esteem evaporated, and taking back the girls no longer seemed to be an option.

From experiencing this period in my life, I came to understand *Battered Women's Syndrome* and how, when we lose enough of our self-esteem, we can no longer make healthy decisions for our life. Instead, we become consumed with feelings of inadequacy and blame.

At midnight, in the first days of September while I was closing the bar where I worked as the assistant manager, I received a call from Eve, announcing that she, Adam, and the girls would be leaving the next morning at 6 A.M. to go to Edmonton, which is six hours north of Lethbridge. "Everything has been arranged," she explained. Adam had landed a fantastic job with a great salary, they had rented a nice house, and they were going to be able to give the kids the best of everything. They were leaving in the morning, and wasn't I excited for them, she asked. She told me that I needed to give them this chance and to not stand in the way of giving the best to the girls; if I loved them, I would "not interfere."

I panicked; I was afraid I would lose them forever, so I said that I would go, too. This would buy me some time to figure things out, I thought. Maybe things would be better in Edmonton. I reasoned that I could not take this opportunity away from them if I loved them. After all, there was nothing and no one to stay in Lethbridge for. I surrendered to the idea, and at 6 A.M. the following morning, I was heading north.

THE BREAKING POINT

Two days after my arrival in Edmonton, I had landed a job at the Edmonton Convention Center Dining Room. I worked there for a week. Then, while driving to my temporary residence after work, I snapped—I literally lost my mind, my memory, use of my nervous system, and my ability to function.

It was 6 P.M. that day, and I sat at the intersection on Jasper Avenue and 103 Street. The light was green, but I didn't know what to do. Drivers were honking their horns at me, wanting me to go. I couldn't, I was dazed—physically immobilized and disoriented. Somehow after a while, I managed to get to a pay phone. I dialled my stepdad's number, and the recording of the operator's voice came on. "You are dialling a long-distance number. Please check the number and try your call again or call the operator for assistance." I tried again, and again got the recording. I was crying, I was afraid. I called the operator explaining that I wanted to talk to my dad. I gave her the number, and she said that I was calling from a pay phone in Edmonton, and the number I was calling was in Lethbridge. I didn't understand; she repeated herself. I was sobbing uncontrollably and so, compassionately, she patched me through, and my stepdad Ron answered the phone.

I rambled on, confused and afraid. Ron said that he had been worried about my compliance with the move to begin with. He said that I had not been myself for months. Ron, who had separated from my mother the previous year, sent for his girlfriend's daughter to pick me up and bring me back to Lethbridge.

The following day, I went to see a doctor, who diagnosed me with nervous exhaustion. I weighed 96 pounds. The doctor explained that all my nerve endings were damaged. This condition was due to high levels of stress, poor nutrition (I was anorexic), and lack of sleep. The doctor explained that the symptoms of this illness would leave my body unable to receive the messages that my brain was sending through my nervous system. I felt drunk without drinking. It took me an enormous effort to pick up a cup or walk; my speech was slurred and drawn out—I was a mess. The doctor said it would take six months to a year to recover.

Two weeks following the good doctor's prognosis, I

wound up in a Catholic church with Ron. I had repeatedly refused to go anywhere near a place of worship, but my stepdad's persistent urgings, his love, and his intuition finally persuaded me to go. The service that Sunday was meant to be a healing service; a bishop who had a very good reputation for healing the sick had come to do "hands-on healings." Exhausted, I surrendered.

The healing service lasted for three hours; I sobbed uncontrollably the whole time. I had not cried since my trip to Calgary months earlier, to be with my baby daughter while she was fighting for her life. It is true that tears and laughter are the true healers of the sick. For years, I had felt that I was much too strong to cry, or so I thought. I have since realized that every tear we are meant to cry, we will cry; the choice is whether we cry them out when they are inspired, or save them up for a downpour.

After the service had ended and not a person was left in the chapel except the bishop, my stepfather carried me (I was unable to walk on my own) to the bishop's chamber and asked if he would pray and do a healing for me. The bishop's eyes swelled with compassion, as he seemed able to look deeply into my heart and soul. He told me to sit; he bowed my head forward and placed his hands on my shoulders, as I wept some more.

After about fifteen minutes, the bishop began to talk to me, describing my past in extreme and accurate detail. He told me that God loved me so much and that I was never alone. He reminded me that God's Holy Spirit was always there for me as a comforter and guide. He continued by saying that this was "my journey," and although there were hard times now and still ahead, the rewards of those hard times would well exceed the trials. Without any input from me, he told me that I needed to change the way I looked at the situation with the girls and Adam and his girlfriend. He insisted that my life was part of a much bigger cosmic plan, and that I needed to keep going. I had much to give the world, he said, but to do so I needed to endure certain experiences. He concluded by saying that I would never be alone, and that my soul was strong and able to handle anything that I needed to bear. "Always remember that you can ask for and receive miracles," he said.

It seemed as though he had, with his last words, somehow commanded miracles into the rest of my life. I was instantly healed; I walked out of that church whole and inspired to continue my sacred journey, whatever it might be.

Reflections on the Dance

Upon reflection of my life, I have come to realize that my childhood had greatly influenced the way I made my decisions based on past experiences. This awareness now helps me to consciously attempt to act from my authentic self rather than function from the perspective of the filters of my past. My core wound continues to be that I often feel as though I were not good enough, no matter how successful others may perceive me to be. I suppose that I came into this life attempting to heal this perception. For my children, I deeply wanted a life that was less trying than mine.

I have gone back in my mind so many times to understand this dance and come to terms with the fact that I could not get out of it, because it, too, was the dance of love. No matter how much I resisted dancing, I can now see clearly that it propelled me forward in my spiritual journey. I was not a bad mother, nor did I abandon my girls. I was the product of a series of events, relationship encounters, and experiences that I had to endure. And, yes, the culmination of challenges did alter my reasoning faculty and self-esteem, but in my heart I know that I did all that I could to sidestep the dance that my soul insisted I do. It was through this experience, and the many subsequent ones, that I learned that soul contracts are bigger than we are in our humanness. Soul contracts are supported by the heart, not by the reasoning faculty of the perceptual mind. In addition, I've repeatedly discovered that the heart will send us on journeys that are unimaginably hard, but have as their primary objective and reward the long-term evolution of the soul.

THE DANCE CONTINUES

It was October 1984, and in just a few short weeks following my healing, I had found an apartment in Edmonton and a new job, and I had moved to be nearer to my girls. I innocently believed that it was the desire of Adam and Eve to include me in the joint parenting agreement we had agreed on just five months earlier. To fulfill my role as the girls' mother, I needed to be sufficiently close geographically. Eve and I had decided from the start that we could set a precedent and demonstrate that even though marriages break apart, individuals could create healthy co-parenting roles. We wanted to set a new paradigm, or so I thought. The goal was to continue to nurture the growth of the children and in doing so, support Adam and Eve's marriage, and to blend family dynamics. In hindsight, I should have paid much closer attention to the fact that Eve had my girls call her "mom" just weeks after they had moved in with her and Adam.

In the six months following my relocation to Edmonton, I began to see the hidden agenda that Adam and Eve had had all along. I learned that Eve had become pregnant weeks prior to their request for shared parenting. She had not expected to have children because of reproductive health problems, but when she "miraculously" became pregnant and realized that she was going to be a mother anyway—why not mother all his children?

Eve confessed 14 years later that she had deduced that since she was pregnant with one child, she might as well have them all! At first, she wanted to try the shared parenting plan, but within weeks of caring for the girls, and feeling resentful towards me, she and Adam had concluded that they could have the "perfect happy family" if I were not around.

What I learned about Eve's childhood early on in our relationship helped me to understand her actions in regard to my girls. When Eve was 13 years old, her mother had died of a brain hemorrhage. From that time onward, she perceived her mom as missing, unattainable, and unavailable for support. She became very angry with God, "for taking [her] mom away." We had this discussion the first time we met, which was four months after she and Adam began their relationship. I had assured her then that her mom was neither missing nor unavailable for her to talk to, although she would need to use her thoughts, rather than her voice, to communicate with her. She discounted both my suggestions. From my encounters with spirit, I knew that Eve's mother lived, was often around her, and loved her daughter dearly, even though Eve was unwilling to believe this.

For Eve, the perceived "absence" of her mom, which began soon after her mom had died, became an unconscious destructive driving force in her psyche. This perceived "void" set into motion a cosmic dance that would in time transform us all. Remember that anything you do not love, because you cannot see the two sides of it, you will ultimately *create, attract,* or *become.* Therefore, Eve was "destined" to repeat what she did not love, namely her perceived abandonment.

Consciously, Eve wanted to change the outcome of her mother's "leaving"; she wanted to have her back, or find some replacement for the void. Unconsciously, she wanted to save anyone who in her mind had become abandoned in some form. First was Adam, then my girls. From her perception, I had abandoned them all, so she could rescue them from the pain she had felt when her mother died.

Consequently, what she seared into the girls' little minds was that I was like her mom in that I had left them, but that she could replace me, so that they didn't have to feel what she had felt. Since in her perception, her mother had abandoned her, she could "save" them from experiencing the pain that she had so deeply felt.

It is important to realize that on a soul level, all these dances were proceeding according to the cosmic plan. I have since come to understand that my girls, Adam, Eve, and I were contracted to do this dance together. The question is, could this dance have been done more caringly? The answer is undoubtedly yes. Are there as many blessings because it wasn't? The answer, again, is yes. And that is the magnificence of the Great Orchestrating Design. No matter what we do, we are loved, and so are those who are affected by our choices. The fact that Adam and Eve were destined to care for my girls was predetermined, but that I needed to be excommunicated from their physical lives was not. Miraculously, however, God ensures and helps us uphold our soul contracts. Simultaneously, the Great Orchestrating Design turns perceived tragedy into blessings and human suffering into spiritual enlightenment–I have come to know this with certainty.

I know that both Adam and Eve are reflections of myself; both sides of me–the part I like and parts I saw as bad or shadowed, that I once kept hidden. Also, I know that we were all simply pursuing what we valued–a family life, the healing of some perceived voids, and true love. I am certain that each of us held particular beliefs that we were to experience and learn to love. I see clearly how everything we resisted loving and seeing the order and magnificence in, we created, attracted, or became. And, lastly, how all of us suffered from self-esteem issues, for the same reason we all do: because we didn't really know who we were, or how truly magnificent we already were.

Now back to the story. Over the sixmonth period I was to live in Edmonton, a "comedy of tragedies" would dance through my life, which set the stage for the next dance.

During the month of November 1985, Eve and I had a volatile hot-and-cold relationship. From the beginning, there had been a strange blending of her wanting my approval and support, and wanting me out of her life. At the time, I was unaware of the reason why she sought my approval. It felt to me like a fatal-attraction relationship. One day, she was pleasant and wanted desperately to be my friend, while the next day, she was feeling abandoned by me and became distant and uncommunicative. I was often on edge and on guard.

On December 22 of the same year, I became violently ill, running dangerously high temperatures, and I fell unconscious for three days. I had contracted the Texas Flu. Adam and Eve ignored my initial pleas for help, and my daughters were told I didn't care about them enough to be with them on Christmas Day, and that they should not expect any Christmas presents from me.

On December 26, I stumbled into the medical clinic in my apartment building, looking for relief from the horrible pain that ravaged through my body. The doctor on call that day was Sam. I could immediately feel his attraction to me, and in the months to follow, we would explore that attraction. At that time, however, all I wanted was pain relief. He prescribed antibiotics and checked on me daily after that.

On December 27, after much pleading from me, Adam and Eve brought the girls over to my place. Grateful and exhausted, I prepared a Christmas dinner for them all, and they opened the presents I had purchased. I had asked to have the girls alone to celebrate what was left of the Christmas season; my request was once again denied.

Because Eve did not trust me, and she was afraid that I would run off with the girls, she never permitted me to take all three at the same time. From the day the girls had moved in with them, I never had all three children alone with me. In spite of prearranged visits of all three girls, there was always an excuse why I could not take one of them, and most of all not Sara. I was too unsuspecting, or naïve, to recognize Eve's game.

Fourteen years later, Eve confessed that she had done

this because she was so afraid that I would run off with the girls. I would not have taken the children from their father, simply because I did not want my children to have to go through the childhood experiences that I had not yet learned to love.

The idea of fleeing conjured all sorts of sad memories of an unhappy childhood for me. I simply could not put my girls through a life of running and hiding, because I knew that Eve, more than Adam, would never give up looking for us. Not only because she loved the girls so much, but because she desperately needed to have my role, as both wife and mother, to heal her unconscious wounds. It would take me 14 years to understand all the reasons why.

In the weeks following my illness, my string of misfortune seemed unending, as my car engine seized up, and the drive train needed extensive repair. The total repair bills added up to thousands of dollars; it took me four months to pay them off.

My car was confiscated until I could pay off most of the bills. The girls lived in Castle Downs, and I lived in downtown Edmonton, approximately 15 kilometres from their home. I could no longer see them unless I took a taxi to their home. I did so every couple of weeks, but that was not enough for Eve, and she began to resent me yet further. My daily absence was used as "proof" that I didn't want the girls.

Times were tough in Edmonton, ever since I had arrived there in October. I worked at two jobs—a lunch shift Monday to Friday, and from 4 P.M. until closing Monday through Saturday, I was a waitress at the Sidetrack Café and Nightclub. By that point in my cosmic journey, I had become both anorexic and bulimic, with my body weight constantly fluctuating by 20 pounds.

When I wasn't working, I either binge ate, starved myself, smoked cigarettes (to curb my insatiable need to feel satisfied), or pedalled away miles and miles on my exercise bike, which I had put on the balcony, since I would burn more calories pedalling in the −15° Celsius temperatures. I was consumed with sorrow, guilt, and self-loathing.

Life for me was, once again, very sad and desperately lonely. The finale of this particular dance occurred in early April, when I was accused of stealing band cover charges from the café where I worked. I pleaded innocence, yet was politely told that I could not continue in this particular job, although I then worked as a kitchen server, where I did not have access to the evening's band cover cash.

By late April, I had decided that the pain and guilt over having given up my children would not end unless I got them back, legally. I felt that if I didn't fight for that opportunity, I would die, emotionally and psychologically, if not physically, since suicide seemed once again like a good way to finally end the pain.

Psychologically, emotionally, and spiritually, I was crucifying myself for ever having believed Eve and Adam about the joint-parenting scenario. I felt betrayed, and I knew that the only way to survive psychologically and emotionally was to "rise up," but how?

The real voyage of discovery consists not in seeking new landscapes, but in having new eyes.

Marcel Proust

CHAPTER 6

My Dances with *Addiction*

I woke up one morning in early May 1986 with a strong feeling that it was time to end my relationship with the doctor who had treated me following the Texas Flu, four months earlier. From January through May, he and I had been spending weekends together. He adored me and would have given the world for my hand in marriage. The financial security he offered would have taken care of all of my problems. But, although I had enjoyed my time with him, I couldn't imagine being his wife. Somehow, this just wasn't in the cards.

That afternoon, I told him I needed to leave Edmonton to go back to Lethbridge to hire a lawyer to fight for the custody of my children. I was embarrassed that I didn't have enough money to fuel up my car for the trip. Lovingly, he gave me a crisp one hundred dollar bill, a hug, and a look of wonder. Somehow in his heart, he knew that I would not be returning; yet in his head, he hoped I would. I said I would pay him back; I never did. I said that I thought I was going to return in a few weeks, but I knew in my heart that I would not.

I arrived back in Lethbridge and, within days, landed another job in a nightclub. A month later, I met my next dance partner, husband number two... (I know you must be wondering how many husbands I've had—the answer is three, and, yes, the third husband and I are still married).

We are contracted to meet certain people at certain times to dance, for reasons unknown at the time. Marsha and I had one such dance to do. We met on the job; we were both working the 8 P.M. to 3 A.M. shift. The owners of the nightclub Who's On Third had hired both of us to attract men to the club. Who's On Third was the hottest new nightclub in the city; it had opened a week earlier.

Marsha and I became fast friends; she needed to get out of a toxic marriage, and I needed a roommate. I counselled her for hours and hours until she finally had the courage to leave her husband. A month after we met, we moved in with her younger sister. Marsha was like an older sister—I was 23, she was 30, and she taught me how to party. Marsha's Dutch family quickly adopted me also; they were a family of seven kids, with wonderfully loving and supportive parents. It was the closest thing to a real family I had ever experienced.

I had retained a lawyer and was suing for shared custody, but wanted to have the day-to-day control of the girls' upbringing. I was working hard to try and keep up with mounting legal bills. Within two months of my move to Lethbridge, Adam, Eve, and the four kids (they had a boy together) relocated from Canmore to Calgary, where Adam had secured a promising position. Their move reduced the distance between my girls and me somewhat, but Adam and Eve were nevertheless determined to keep me out of the girls' lives. I would travel the three-and-a-half hours regularly, only to be refused entry into their home when I knocked.

By this time, Eve felt so betrayed and abandoned by me that she would not allow me to enter their house—even when my visits had been prearranged. I did not realize then that I was the mother she craved to have back, while all *I* wanted was my girls. The more I wanted them, and not her, the worse things got. Each time I did not do as she expected, wasn't friendly enough, or was delayed from a visit we had arranged, the rage increased. Finally, she began acting strangely and hysterically. There was much more going on than either Adam or I understood.

When she would refuse me to see the girls, I would go the hotel where Adam worked and wait all evening until he went home, so I would be able to see the girls for a couple of hours before I had to head home for another shift. By then, even Adam wondered about the psychological health of his fiancée. He said that she had begun imagining things, and believed me to be stalking their home. From his standpoint, the less I was around, the better she did. Total alienation was imminent.

In spite of my determination to get my girls back, I was still deeply addicted to all sorts of things such as food, alcohol, cigarettes, sex, and, through a new contact at the nightclub, "speed," otherwise known as "little white crosses." Little white crosses are prescription diet pills that increase mental alertness. Truckers are known to be frequent users. What they were called didn't matter to me, though, as long as I had a full supply. The pills picked me up, emotionally and psychologically, but most of all, they kept me going when nothing else I tried worked. I bought a thousand pills for $75.

I was still obsessed with my weight, and wanted someone to love, yet felt it impossible at my perceived obese weight of 138 pounds. I am five-foot-two, and although 138 pounds was more than I cared to be, it was a long way from obese, yet that is exactly how I felt.

Soon, alcohol, sex, cigarettes, cocaine, magic mushrooms, and cannabis were all on my "will-this-work-to-get-rid-of-the-pain?" list, but only the little white crosses worked, so I hung on to them desperately.

A month after starting at Who's On Third, I met my husband number two. Jake came into the bar daily, shot four or five hours of pool (he was good), and downed several jugs of draft beer. We flirted, and then finally one day he asked me out. Like attracts like, and two months later, we were living together, both addicted, both in pain, and in love, or so we thought.

We were perfect dance partners, for a while, and then I asked him to stop drinking. Of course, I was still taking "speed" daily (he never knew). In fact, I was taking six pills twice a day, when the prescribed dose was one for every twelve-hour period. No one knew how addicted I had become, and no one knew I was taking "speed" daily.

In February 1987, I discovered I was pregnant. I was

ecstatic, but terrified to think of what the "speed" might have done to the baby. Jake and I were living in Thunder Bay, Ontario, at the time, where we would be staying for approximately six weeks. My next decision was obvious—I needed to say goodbye to the drugs. And, with a prayer of gratitude for being given a second chance and a precious new soul to mother, I flushed 776 pills down the toilet. Three weeks later, I miscarried.

I wanted a new beginning more than the drugs. I wanted to prove that I was a good mom, more than I wanted the drugs. And I needed to prove to everyone, but most of all to myself, that I had not abandoned the girls. In surrendering the drugs, I felt I would prove just that. However, the "speed" had all but destroyed my metabolism, and without the drugs to make me "feel good," life became unmanageable.

This time, help came in two distinct ways: One was a book that supported me in the world of the physical, and months later, a spirit guide in the world of the spiritual. Helen is one of my spirit guides—you will meet her in chapter seven. The book was *The Power of Your Subconscious Mind* by Joseph Murphy. I read it over and over; it became my new bible.

This book talked about intention, meditation, visualization, and healing. It suggested that I could heal myself with my mind. I believed, and I meditated for hours and hours; it was the only thing I had left to be addicted to. Weeks turned into months, and somehow, without medical intervention, my mind, body, and spirit were integrating again. I was slowly, slowly, getting well.

From my ongoing work with addiction, I have come to discover some tools that have aided many clients, as they aided me on the long road of addiction that so many of us travel. On the deepest level, addiction is driven by our desire to know the Great Orchestrating Design, or love. To be in a relationship with love also means to be in a relationship with ourselves. Since the ego, or separated mind, desperately wants us to avoid finding ourselves and the truth of our being, addiction is one of its primary arsenals to keep us searching but never finding peace and joy–the outcome we hope for whenever we ingest any substance that we expect will make us feel good.

Interestingly, peace and joy are also the natural states that emanate from truth and our authentic being as spirit. The primary difference in experiencing peace and joy through natural means is that these feelings are reflective rather than objective. Consequently, substances and external fixes of any kind that are pursued to make us feel good serve as masks to obscure our deeper desire to know our heritage and being.

The journey of addiction seems to be a path we will all travel in order to become enlightened and increase consciousness. Addiction serves us to increase our power in two primary areas–one is a heightened willpower and the other is our awesome yet terrifying power of choice.

Willpower and choice must be applied to free oneself from addiction. If they are not applied, then the stage is set for the potential abuse of "substances," which can include insatiable yearnings towards people, substances, rituals, foods, sex, shopping, and actions such as biting nails, and so on. Magically, the experience of addictive behavior also serves as a mirror of some of our deepest authentic natures that are not yet fully understood, such as the desire for anything we perceive as missing, and the satisfaction of the fulfillment of that desire.

Through examining addictive patterns, we enlighten ourselves as we become aware that we have an incessant want to feel good. What we are unaware of is that, in reality, we also feel bad at the same time as we feel good, but that the "feeling bad" is hidden, because the part of the mind that is searching is separated off from its other side. The separated mind can see only one side at a time. However, when an individual is asked to find the bad, it will usually show up to the amazement of the person. The bad may show up in the same area as the good or in another. For instance, I may be feeling good because I received a great book review, and then when I look for the bad, which was present at the same time as the good came, I may find it in the realization that I also felt bad because I hadn't spoken to my children for days. The next bad book review might simultaneously bring with it the memory of the good one. The important thing to notice in either case is that the good and bad come as a pair. The point that is imperative to understand is that both bad and good are inseparable.

Addiction is driven by two components—the desire to know God and the fixation to separate pairs that are inseparable. All traits and qualities, such as hot and cold, up and down, pain and pleasure, are born from the dual nature of two opposites. Together, they make up light, consciousness, and physical life itself.

Unknowingly we yearn for love, feelings, and events to be one-sided because we have not yet understood the benefits of having both sides of anything simultaneously. Yet, as Einstein stated, "The will of God is equilibrium," and this truth can also be applied to the world of addiction. Once we can honestly view the balancing factors in the areas we once felt guilty and incompetent in, addictive patterns start to disintegrate.

Since each side of anything comes paired to its opposite, the desire to separate the two fuels the addiction itself. Wanting pleasure to avoid pain is the desire that drives the addictive pattern. Unendingly and despairingly, we try to experience one half of the pair, until one day we realize that bliss becomes the medicine available to us through the appreciation of these inseparable pairs in our life. Bliss then finally becomes our choice of ointment on our once perceived separated self. Bliss, we discover, is our natural state of being and always available to us, without consuming externals of any kind. Bliss, we learn, is a state that encompasses all opposites and is available to us through the appreciation of these opposite "inseparables." Eventually, we rise above the avoidance of the pain/pleasure dynamic to find ourselves liberated to choose that which reflects our being, rather than to avoid it.

Since in reality, there is nothing in or of the material world that can quench our deepest yearning to know ourselves and thus God, the path of addiction is paved with pursuits until we recognize there is nothing missing, or out of accord, in our lives. We surrender to the fact that all external yearnings took the mask of something that could seemingly fix someone not broken. To the extent that we are able to keep truth intact within our awareness, we are able to stop the wheel of suffering from spinning in our lives. As we awaken to the fact that bliss must come from who we are, rather than who we fantasize we ought to be, our peace of mind is restored.

The following is a reflection on a particularly intense alcoholic experience by Jordan, one of my students and an aspiring writer:

May 6th

Looking back to my misadventures on May 6, which include being heavily intoxicated and losing possession of my most treasured journal writings, I can identify two very obvious and basic lessons:

First of all, the entire day was a perfect example of how the universe mirrors your attitude towards it. It flawlessly develops situations in accordance with how you present yourself to it, and then how you negotiate every opportunity that is bestowed upon you. If you look close enough at any situation that is thought to be unfortunate or negative, it is clear that there is always the chance to switch things around in your favor, ultimately gaining yourself wisdom and understanding. If you squander these moments, the universe will continue to let you slip in that particular direction until you can see the rewards of it and flip yourself around. It will provide all the support needed to help you see that you have the power to get exactly what you put into anything attempted in life, whether it is destructive or productive.

Second, it is a simple fact that under the influence of any mind-altering substance, you aren't present and can't function at an optimal level of awareness. It was not just missing my plane and losing my binder full of journal notes at the Calgary airport that frustrated me. The entire day seemed to be filled with flaws and pointless events, all of which turned out to be a great big learning curve. *These events were an example of the law of the one and the many. What this meant for me was that one drink turned into many. It showed me how powerless I can let myself become over a simple pleasure that, when analyzed, isn't a pleasure at all. Following some contemplation on the plane to Seattle, I was reminded of how dangerous it is when I push myself to the point of complete blackout. I have realized that I don't need to push myself very hard to end up in a blackout situation. It seems blackouts and I come hand in hand once I've begun to drink.*

I don't really know how life will be tomorrow, or in a year, or in five years. I would like to guess at where and what I will be, but all I know for sure is where and what I am right now. All I can believe at this moment is the old saying, "Life is a journey, not a destination." There is this little voice telling me that there is more to the equation than the quote above. I have yet to know.

Jordan Korth, May 12, 2004

CHAPTER 7

Turbulence and Trial

Following our brief stay in Ontario, and then a five-month stint in Fort Nelson, BC, I insisted that Jake and I go south to be closer to the girls, yet not so close as to make Adam and Eve move farther away, as they had done so many times before. So, in April 1987, Jake and I moved farther south to Port Alberni on Vancouver Island. This was to be our home for the next 18 months.

In the first few months of settling into our new home, I became resentful of Jake. He worked during the day and spent many hours during the night drinking. Soon, I began to rage inwardly, then I started whining to him about his behavior, then I shut down completely. I was hurting terribly inside because of the continued geographical distance between me and my children, and the realization that I was in a relationship with an alcoholic.

In my childhood days, I had learned the practice of meditation. Later, while repeatedly reading *The Power of the Subconscious Mind*, I was again reminded of the importance of meditating. I remembered how meditation had given me a sense of inner peace when I had practiced it regularly. Therefore, I decided that if I wanted to change my feelings and outcomes, I should take up meditation again, since nothing I did outwardly seemed to help heal the deep inner pain that I was feeling.

Then, one day while meditating, and quite by surprise, an elderly lady with silver-blond hair appeared in my mind. She introduced herself as Helen, and she would soon become a constant friend and companion, when I thought no one else was there to turn to. Helen told me that, as long as I blamed others for my feelings and experiences, they would imprison me. Sternly yet lovingly, she taught me day after day that Jake, Adam, or Eve were not the problem, but rather, that I was the problem. She taught me all about perception, and reminded me that my ego didn't matter in what my spirit knew about the grand plan of my life. In response to the insights she offered, I would naturally recede and contemplate their wisdom. She often repeated that, as long as I had expectations of how others should be, I would be disappointed. "People aren't just in your life as you want them to be, dear," she said. "They are there for you to appreciate, for all that they offer you."

At first I thought she was crazy, I didn't understand, or rather, I didn't remember what I knew as a child, which was exactly what she had stated. Early on, I knew that people were in our life to appreciate and grow with, not to condemn, so why had I forgotten?

Daily, during our dialogues, she showed me that if I could love Jake as he was, then one day, he would become what I wanted him to be. I practiced being kinder and gentler, and soon the relationship between us turned around.

THE TRIAL

During that year, I would travel back and forth to Calgary countless times to meet with my lawyer to prepare for my divorce trial. By October 1987, I was four months pregnant with Jake's and my son. I was staying in Lethbridge with my dear friend Marsha and driving to Calgary twice a week, anxiously fighting for visitation rights to the girls, who had become extremely hostile as a result of the "programming" against me. Vigilantly, my lawyer and I prepared the evidence for the custody trial ahead.

I sat through discovery after discovery, stunned by the apparent hostility and hatefulness Adam and Eve displayed towards me. This was coupled with a storybook of lies and deceitful evidence that would not eventually stand up in court. Adam and Eve regularly failed to comply with court-ordered visitations I had been granted in the six months prior to trial. My only form of recourse had been to call the police to go to their home to enforce the court order, so I could spend some time with my girls. Of course, from the children's standpoint, their perception had been that I was being mean by calling the police against their parents. One of the most extreme accusations made about me during the pretrial period was an accusation of sexual and physical abuse against Sara, following her having an allergic reaction to blueberries. Eve was often quick to jump to the most outrageous or hurtful of conclusions.

Jake and I were married 18 months after we met. Our whole relationship revolved around my wanting to get my girls back–and his struggle with gambling and alcohol. Our relationship was riddled with hurdles from the start, offering us both tremendous opportunities to grow. Jake needed to earn some quick cash to pay his three years' arrears in income taxes, and I needed big money to pay my divorce lawyer. Individually, we both had unresolved issues with parents and with self-worth. I came into his life in part to help him find his way as an individual apart from his two older brothers, who, for the most part, had "fathered" him since Jake's dad had died when he was young. Jake came into my life to show me I was still worthy of love, and to financially support me while I focused on regaining a relationship with my girls. It was a gift I am grateful for to this day.

During the last leg before the trial, I was pregnant and unable to work due to the demands of living in Lethbridge temporarily and preparing for court in Calgary. As I had no income at the time, I was no longer able to pay for the growing legal fees. Heartbroken at the thought that I would have to give up because of monetary issues, I asked for help. Help came graciously, through my lawyer, Karen, who decided it would be a moral injustice to give up, when she knew in her heart that, unless she took action, I would lose all chances of a relationship with my three young children.

Karen pleaded my case to the partners of her firm and offered to do the remainder of the work ahead "pro bono." She was just fresh out of law school and knew in her heart that this was a case worth fighting for. "It was the reason I went into family law to begin with," Karen told me. "Your only responsibility from here on in is to cover the administrative costs in-curred by me in order to continue representing you," she said. With tear-filled eyes, I gratefully agreed. Upon completion of this trial, I was made aware that the total cost of the trial had been in excess of $100,000, an amount that was absorbed by many different parties. The portion that I was liable for was a small price to pay for the wisdom I gained, and the love that I experienced from my lawyer.

By December 1987, we finally got to court, and the key assessment to be made was whether or not my girls had been programmed to fear and hate me, and this was appropriately referred to as "Parent Alienation Syndrome." Days before the trial, the children announced, "You should just go away—we have a new mommy now, we don't want to be with you."

As a part of the process of determining the truth, my lawyer insisted that we have complete bilateral psychological assessments done, which means assessments of all parental figures and of each child. She chose one of the most respected and knowledgeable psychologists in the city. It took him six weeks to determine, from the extensive visits and psychological tests, who was the better parent. Adam and Eve's lawyer had unilateral assessments done as well, which meant that only the two of them were assessed. I never met with the psychologist they saw in the unilateral assessment, yet in court he discussed, for 20 minutes, my personality traits and what he felt my relationship with my daughters was like.

The evidence from the bilateral assessment was that extensive brainwashing had been going on for years. "The children demonstrated unusually high levels of animosity towards their natural mother," noted the comments in the bilateral report. "Even when working with children who were actually physically abused, I had never seen such angry and unforgiving children," the doctor testified. He spoke about how defensive the girls were of their new "mom," while calling their natural mother by her first name. He said that he found what he saw "greatly disturbing." Then he turned his attention towards the judge and stated that, "strange dynamics were underway between the two mothers." To summarize, he believed that the natural mother was seen as a dangerous threat to the acting stepmom and that he had serious concerns about the stepmother's mental health. He mentioned that the stepmother's mother had died when she was thirteen, and felt that there were serious unresolved abandonment issues that she was unconsciously dealing with. In light of the death of her mother, and the unresolved abandonment felt by the stepmother, the doctor indicated that she was unconsciously "rescuing" these little girls in order to heal her own abandonment issue.

Next, the psychologist turned his attention to the father of the children, Adam. He had concluded that he was subservient to the overwhelming emotional needs of his fiancée. It seemed very apparent that it was primarily the stepmother who was the initiator of most of the blending family problems. The psychologist stated that even the father had picked up on some "strange jealousy and envy that she portrayed towards the natural mother."

The father had indicated to him that Eve "fluctuated between wanting the natural mother out of their lives, and wanting her friendship and approval, while simultaneously wanting her acknowledgment to show that she had taken over for her when she had 'abandoned them.'"

The children were not asked to testify; they were 7, 6, and 4 years old. The days dragged on, with a stream of character witnesses that Adam and Eve had brought in, in order to bash my character. Many of them I did not know. Then, after four heart-wrenching days, it was finally over, and it was my turn to respond.

It took the stand at 9 A.M. and presented my side, which was that I felt cheated by them. All of this had happened because I had trusted in their intention to co-parent. I had never abandoned my girls. The physical evidence of phone bills, a medical report, engine repairs, etc., substantiated the circumstances that I was always committed to being in their life as their mother. I also spoke of the heart-wrenching feelings I had to endure every time I went to their house to see my girls. I shared how hard it was to see that I had been so easily "replaced." I admitted that my emotional, psychological, and physical well-being had taken huge hits in the past three years, but that I felt certain I was well enough to care for the girls. I spoke to the judge and recognized how the times that I was unable to visit the girls, due to extreme circumstances, would have been very hard on Eve and the girls equally. I also reminded of the countless times that I was refused visitation. I admitted that the past years had been tough on all of us, but that I was committed to doing things right now. I suggested that if I were awarded joint custody, I would uphold what was best for the girls, putting the past behind us. I knew I was capable of supporting access to the girls by the four acting parents in their lives. I concluded by asking the judge to do what he felt was best for the girls, to provide stability. If he felt that my girls would do best, in light of all the programming, with my former husband, Adam, then I would sadly comply, provided I had access to them at least a third of the year. I pleaded for his wisdom in what would shape the future of our lives. I was then cross-examined for one-and-a-half hours.

The next person to be cross-examined was Jake. He talked about wanting to start a new life with me and our soon-to-be-born child. He said that he was happy to act as a stepfather, but that he couldn't stand the fighting anymore. He spoke about how hard it was on our relationship to go through all of this. Jake said that he could no longer watch me cry and grieve for my girls. He told the judge that the thought of my getting another chance to prove my worthiness as a mother, in that I would be able to show my love and devotion to our child, was all that kept him going. He indicated that we would start over in British Columbia. He said he loved it there, and thought it would be a great place to raise children.

Then my stepdad, Ron, testified. He spoke about the incredibly difficult life that I had had. He said that he didn't know a stronger or more loving mother. He said he knew that Eve loved the girls, but often wondered about her motive. He indicated that if I had died, she would have been a wonderful fill-in, but this was not the case, and Eve seemed unclear of the appropriate boundaries to her role in the girls' lives. He told the judge that he knew I would never run off with the kids because my childhood had been so painful as a result of child abduction, and that we had spent years hiding from my father and later from social services. He said that if anyone would be able to put the past behind them and do what was most loving for her kids, I would. He apologized for not being there more for me, but stated to the court that he, too, was fighting against his former wife, my mother, for the custody of his son. Ron was the last witness; the trial was finally over, and we awaited judgment.

Affidavit upon affidavit, and stacks of evidence and psychological reports were waiting for the judge to review. Finally, after five days of trial and character-bashing from Adam and Eve's side, and our half-day rebuttal supplying physical evidence for the love and commitment I had always shown the girls, the decision was given.

In my testimony, I had asked the judge to do what he felt best for the children—for their best outcome in the future, given all the evidence.

In his statement, the judge reprimanded Adam and Eve for their appalling and so apparent behavior in the courtroom and in the previous years. He then continued by saying he felt that if I lived in Calgary, where the children resided, he would have awarded me the day-to-day care and control. However, because this was not the case, and considering the geographic distance, coupled with the many years of estrangement and parent alienation that the girls had suffered, he felt that it was in their best interest to continue residing with the father, but that a very detailed list of access times to the children was being prepared and that if, at any time, access were denied again, he would immediately order the change in custody, care, and control. The judge closed the case, suggesting that I should come back to see him if there were further issues with Adam and Eve. I never did get an opportunity to do this, however, because he retired a year after the case closed.

Reflections on the Dance

Most of us have the belief that if you are a good person, then only good things should happen to you. And alternatively, if you are a bad person, ultimately bad things will happen to you. From the many difficulties I experienced throughout my life, I learned that this is a self-limiting, judgmental, and mistaken belief. What is good or bad depends upon who is discerning it, based upon individual ideals, values, and beliefs.

We tend to become fearful when, though we are comfortable doing the more common dances, we are expected to leap in our learning and become skilled at the intricate steps of a more complex dance—a dance that we feel is painfully hard to learn, but which, if danced by the seasoned master, who demonstrates it's possible to accomplish, we also marvel at.

We are all masters, and we are here to learn each and every experience, or dance, that reveals love's power. We eventually do all the dances necessary to evolve. As a result of incorporating every step of each of the dances, we will eventually be able to aid others in doing them also; and through our first doing them, followed by integrating them, we will know with certainty, as does the master, the gratitude that is present in their accomplishment.

To the soul, the path that is pursued most diligently is the one that will teach us how to love most fully and honestly. The soul will embark upon the dance floor, which is certain to attract those partners who will most reflect both loved and unloved parts of itself. Magically, then, we will each come to learn that moving in and through love does not mean self-sacrifice; rather it means that the self becomes more expansive, encompassing all our dance partners. Through dances like these, we become truthful enough to see that no one really betrays anyone, but is instead only pursuing what each values and appreciates, just as we do.

Great people—who we all are—need to grow through difficult transformative experiences in order to digest the power and wisdom that these occurrences bring. Once these experiences are integrated, understood, and loved (meaning they are seen and appreciated from both sides, and for all involved), we have the power to transform other individuals' perceptions, too.

We often choose a friend as we do a mistress;
for no particular excellence in themselves,
but merely from some circumstance
that flatters our self-love.

William Hazlitt

CHAPTER 8

Yearning for Home

THE GYPSY RETURNS

Soon it would be Christmas, and I had no money to spare. I needed to buy gifts for the girls, and I dearly wanted to give presents to Jake to give expression to my newfound understanding of who he was and to show kindness towards him. I didn't know what to do. I thought that if I didn't get gifts for the girls, they would think I had stopped caring. I was desperate, and I was determined to get gifts.

I remembered what Mom had taught me about stealing—it's okay as long as you exchange things for things. I gathered some "things" from my belongings, which included toiletries, trinkets, and clothing. I found a shopping bag, stuffed everything into it, and went shopping. I stole doggie slippers and boxers for Jake, some dolls and clothes for the girls, and confidently walked out of the store. Who would have known that all the years of shadowing Mom would someday allow me to give my family a little bit of Christmas? Because I still needed more presents, I went through my grooming supplies next, and polished and cleaned up my curling iron, hairclips, and hairpins, as well as some old ornaments, and boxed everything up and sent it to the girls. I called them a few days later and was happy to hear of their joy at all the surprises. If I had to go to hell or jail, I thought it was worth it—after all, I needed them to know I cared. For several years, I would pray for forgiveness. In my heart, I knew I had stolen. I vowed to atone by going back some day and telling the store what I had done. I never actually did this, but have consciously given in many ways since, to show my gratitude to the Great Orchestrating Design for looking the other way!

The yearning in my heart to be with my girls was softened with the swelling of my pregnant abdomen. Soon I would have another child, one I would cling to devotedly, one that would know I was a great mom, with so much love to give. My first son, Joe, was born in March of 1988. In the months that followed, Jake and I were settling into family life. Jake was a proud father; his life had new meaning, as did mine.

By June of that same year, I was preparing for the arrival of my three girls to spend a month's holiday with Jake, their new baby brother, and myself in Port Alberni. On July 1, I arrived in Calgary by Greyhound Bus to pick them up. I was so proud to travel with them; I was only 24 years old and fulfilling my maternal role beautifully. Most people were surprised when they heard the children call me "mom." They were astonished by my procreative abilities and by my ease and confidence as a young mother of so many.

That month flew by quickly. The girls were happy to be with me; in fact, no one who saw us together would have believed that a separation had ever occurred. The girls were in many ways *at home*.

Eve called every day, sometimes twice. She had recently become a born-again Christian and was deeply concerned for the safety of the girls' souls while they were in my presence. She became more and more uneasy with each passing day and began to question my parenting skills from a distance.

The girls changed when they spoke to her on the phone; they became quiet and agreed to do everything she requested, such as prayers before each meal and before bed, drawing pictures for her, and talking to Jesus when they missed her. Once the phone was hung up, however, they did as they pleased, disregarding all of Eve's requests; they returned to being guilt-free, spirited children.

I imagine that Eve was terrified and afraid that they might want to stay with me, and by the end of the month, my oldest daughter, Emma, wanted just that. Adam and Eve refused, made Emma feel guilty for asking, and shut down all considerations of her request.

The month ended and my girls left; again my heart was left aching for more time, more hugs, and more mothering. This was the final straw for me. From that day forward, I told Jake it was not a matter of if, but when, we would return to Calgary, so I could share in their lives, too.

I stayed focused on Joe, because he was what kept me going, when so many times I wanted to give in. In previous years, there were many times when taking matters into my own hands seemed rational. Now I had Joe to keep clear and focused for; I needed a plan in order to get home.

Weekly, I urged Jake to move back to Alberta with me. He resisted; he loved British Columbia—he loved the trees; he loved fishing; he loved his son; he had no reason to go back.

His increase in gambling and drinking distanced us. Soon I began getting angry, then shutting down, then going numb—just as I had done earlier during the custody trial. I began pressing harder and harder to leave, until one day I told him I was going with or without him. Then, by a stroke of luck, his work turned sour; he decided that he was no longer content with his employers and the dollars they paid him for his work as a journeyman flooring installer.

A Miracle Baby Boy

I had been feeling pregnant for weeks, so I went to the doctor to confirm my feelings. He ran pregnancy tests, and they came back negative. Weeks passed, and again I insisted that I was pregnant; the doctor ran more tests, and again the results were negative. This was my sixth pregnancy—I knew my body, and I knew I was pregnant, no matter what the results said.

It was midwinter when Jake's brother Tom came for a visit. I immediately had concerns, because I knew that Tom was also drinking. Soon after Tom's arrival, the bottle of rye was opened, and it wasn't long before he and Jake were fighting and becoming physical. A full-blown show of fists to cuffs broke out; I was worried and called the police. The officers who came convinced Jake and Tom to settle down and go to bed. Soon after both men had gone to sleep, I began to feel a severe pain in my abdomen. When there was no improvement after a couple of hours, I drove myself to the hospital to see what was happening.

I told the nurse that I had been feeling pregnant for months, but that the results had kept coming back negative. I told her that I felt like I wanted to push, the pain was overwhelming. She asked when I had last eaten; I told her about three hours earlier. She called for a physician. It was 2 A.M.

I was sent for an ultrasound. "Oh, wow!" said the technician, but wouldn't tell me what she had seen. I needed to wait for the doctor. I asked if I was going to live. "Oh gosh, yes. It's not something that we can't fix," she said. She told me that I would get the results within 15 minutes.

Next, they called Jake, because there was a small chance that my life was in danger. He was told, even before they told me, that they suspected a tubal pregnancy, which would require an operation right away. I was prepped for surgery. I told the doctor that I was pregnant. He nodded, and I fell asleep.

When I awoke the next morning, I was told that I had a cyst the size of a grapefruit in my uterus. The cyst was bleeding, and I had been feeling the pressure of the accumulated blood. Later that morning, the surgeon came into my room and announced that I was, in fact, pregnant, but that the cyst had altered the hormonal balance and that was the reason the tests had come back negative. He said there was almost no chance that the pregnancy could continue. The cyst had been on the left ovary, while the right had produced the ovum. With such invasive surgery in the first three months of pregnancy, it would be a miracle if the fetus survived. He advised me not to hold out any hope. I knew in my heart that all was going to be fine. (Six months later, I would indeed give birth to a healthy baby boy—my second son, Jeremy.)

MOVING TO ALBERTA

In the months following the operation, Jake had been conversing with his oldest brother, Wes, in Taber, Alberta. Wes and their middle brother, Tom, owned a flooring store in Taber. Wes spoke of a good partnership opportunity in the company. "The three amigos running the store and doing installs would be a great idea," Wes suggested. Wes urged Jake to move, and a few months later, in May 1989, we did.

We found an interim home until July, when we moved to "the little green house," a name the girls coined shortly after their second visit. I saw the girls almost every other weekend. I would pack up Joe and drive from Taber to Calgary. The round trip took me almost five hours. I loved being nearer to the girls, and I thought that the hard times were behind us now, but I was mistaken.

The following year was very hard on my relationship with Jake. He and both his brothers loved drinking and gambling. When he was not drinking, gambling, or working, he was absorbed in Nintendo games. I began working nights as a bartender to help support the family.

Jake watched the boys, Joe and Jeremy, then aged 20 months and two months.

Working together turned out to be harder for the three brothers than they had expected. Gambling drove Tom to embezzlement from the company, and Jake soon decided that he wanted to get out of the family mess. In May of 1990, we finally moved to Calgary; my prayers were answered.

Reflections on the Dance

What I learned from this epoch is that no matter how far we climb, there is always another mountain around the corner to keep us ascending. Each mountain offers a particular set of illusions and truths to climb over. Each mountain conquered then begins the level from which the next climb begins.

We tend to run our lives believing that we would be happy "if only"...attaching an endless string of conditions. Nevertheless, the accomplishment of any goal seems somewhat less rewarding than it originally appeared to be. We each set up an ideal set of values in our minds, believing that life will be perfect when we achieve them. When we attain these values, the next set of wants and perceived needs steps up to greet us.

The void of not having my girls close to me drove my actions toward the attainment of that goal. Once accomplished, however, the next void sprang forth, namely a better marriage, a home that we owned, and financial freedom. It would be those perceived voids that would set the stage for the next dance.

Just let go. Let go of how you thought your life should be
and embrace the life that is trying
to work its way into your consciousness.

Caroline Myss

CHAPTER 9

On My Own Again

It was the summer of 1990 when Jake's and my marriage ended. As much as six months earlier, I had become resigned to the realization that my values were becoming more and more distanced from Jake's, and there was more and more work involved in connecting his needs to my own. I no longer wanted to watch him drink and play video games–I wanted a companion. Consequently, I had begun working additional nights to get away, and on nights that I did not work, I called a friend who was a singer and would go to watch her band perform in local nightclubs. When I returned home, usually around midnight, Jake would be furious. Accusations of my being unfaithful streamed forth from his drunken perception, coupled with his long-standing jealousy issues, which had begun long before I entered his life. For many of these reasons, the weekend we separated was not at all a difficult experience for either of us, as we both seemed to have a clear picture of a better life ahead.

For little Joe, however, the pain was overwhelming. Our son was heartbroken after our separation. I would have never imagined that a child so young could understand so much. He constantly asked for daddy to come home, and for me to not go to work. What he could not understand was that the relationship between his parents had become toxic and abusive because of his dad's preferred lifestyle.

Jeremy, who was just a year old, didn't react at all. However, the guilt I felt every time Joe clung to my leg or came running after me as I left for work was excruciating.

I found the strength to remain separated only because I believed in my heart that the boys had the right to witness a healthy, loving relationship. I wanted them to have a different childhood experience than I had had.

My relationship with the girls was becoming increasingly strained, because Eve was again trying to impose her values and parenting beliefs on me. She regularly called Social Services to report my mothering style and to ask if I was abusing my children, for a myriad of reasons. One of these reasons was that I allowed Joe to go to the play park, which was in the centre of the condo development we lived in, all by himself.

In all fairness, I do admit that I was a trusting, liberal mom. I was not run by the "what ifs" of life. I had a clear sense of intuition that I listened to and trusted. This drove Eve crazy; she was the polar opposite to me in all her "mother" applications—she represented my unexpressed self, as I represented hers. I did not impose my mothering skills on her, so why did she feel she had to impose hers on me? I asked this question after each call I would receive following my weekend or Wednesday evening visits with the girls.

By September of 1991, I was moving again. This was a little move across the road to a lower-income housing complex, where I would live for two years. During this period, I worked, I dated, and I rode the roller coaster of Eve's emotions. The girls were steadily becoming more demanding and judgmental towards me. They were beginning to feel more and more anxious about their visits, because both Adam and Eve were so cold and evasive when they returned.

Because the girls were getting the gears at home for coming to see me, they began to take out their feelings on me. Speaking out to their parents about their feelings of being torn apart was unimaginable, because of the parents' controlling, manipulative, and disciplinary behavior. Adam and Eve had been telling them for years that they needed to decide which parent they wanted, because having both me and their dad freely in their life was out of the question. Eve had been telling them that, if any one of them wanted to live with me, they would have to say goodbye to their other siblings. For my girls, this threat increased the "cost" of living with me. Steadily, they were becoming more and more afraid of challenging these conditions, and the idea of changing homes some day became more and more unthinkable for them.

Soon, Sara no longer came for visits with me, although Emma and Tasha still did. Eve always had a different excuse. Sara, who only ever remembered Eve as her mother, had bonded tightly; she was the easiest of the three girls for Eve to control.

Forcing Sara would have only aggravated an already volatile situation. I had long since learned that diplomacy and nonthreatening action got me further ahead than did force. I just reminded Sara that I loved her and was there if she wanted to come.

From Sara's perspective, she wanted to make Eve happy, and since Eve would cry as she got the girls ready to visit me, Sara deduced that if she stayed with Eve, she could make her mommy "happier." Gratefully, Eve's tears did not work as well on the other two, Emma and Tasha.

The months that followed became more difficult; I was again losing self-confidence, feeling unlovable and unwanted as I moved from relationship to relationship. All I wanted was a good guy, someone whom I could trust, and someone who saw my goodness and wanted to have a loving relationship. By Christmas of 1992, I realized that I was again losing my girls. Scheduled visits were not being kept. I saw them only about once a month.

This year, it was my turn to have Christmas with the girls. I had not had them on Christmas Day since before they went to live with their dad, in spite of the fact that, according to the decision of the trial judge, I was to have them every other Christmas. In fact, I did not get them for even half of my awarded time. I was too tired to fight in court again, and I knew that the influence Adam and Eve had over the girls was much more psychological than physical. I knew that when push came to shove, the girls would again side with them, so again I surrendered. The impact that Adam and Eve had was shown to me when, on my scheduled Christmas visit, Emma called to say that she and her sisters were staying with Adam and Eve instead. I was heartbroken, but not surprised. On the following Wednesday visit, they uncaringly und unappreciatively tore open the gifts still sitting under the tree. It was not the Christmas I had yearned to have with them.

There is nothing absent,
everything is present, already in potential.

Lopon Tenzin Namdak

CHAPTER 10

A Return to Love

It was January 1993, and I was preparing to go to work, when I flicked on *Oprah*. She was talking about a book that she felt was the best book she had ever read–she said it had the power to change a person's life forever. The book was titled *A Return to Love*. As she spoke, I began to feel animated, a slight surge of what felt like electricity began flowing through my body. I felt inspired and joyful, but could not really explain why. Then Oprah introduced her special guest, Marianne Williamson. Marianne was quick to acknowledge that her book was a synthesis of her study of a spiritual text titled *A Course In Miracles*, or simply "the Course." She referred to it continually; my sense from hearing her reverence for its wisdom was that only "special people" could read it; in my perception, I was not then special enough.

I listened, and watched Marianne discuss how many people's problems stemmed from a lack of self-awareness and self-love, coupled with a limiting belief of what love really was, and from confusing infatuation with love. I could relate to that. She continued by sharing that it was a person's perception that could make or break the person's experience or understanding of their life. Then I watched Marianne pray on national TV with a family that was struggling with their differing values and opinions. She did not pray for change; she prayed for a miracle—a change for each in their understanding of the differences they were experiencing. From that instant, I was hooked. I went out that day and bought the book.

I devoured it and began applying its principles vigilantly. I spent countless hours dialoguing with Helen and the Holy Spirit, making sense of the relationships I was involved in at that time.

Desperate Love

At around the time I received the book, I befriended a man named Peter. He had just separated from his wife days before we met. I met him at work, and he needed a shoulder to lean on while he came to terms with the fact that his marriage had ended. I counselled him for hours on end on the theories I was extracting from Marianne's book—he was my test subject, so to speak.

On one occasion, Peter invited me to his house to meet his friend Phil. Peter had a great house, and I wondered why any woman would leave all this. Well, the thought itself became an invitation to see that money can't buy love.

Things felt suspicious; I felt as if his wife was not really gone yet. I wandered upstairs to look at the closet, and saw that it was full of women's clothing. Peter found me standing there, looking at his wife's clothes—I asked why he had lied, and he said that he hadn't lied, that she would be there on the weekend to pick the clothes up. I began to feel uncomfortable and wanted to walk away, when he grabbed me and started kissing me. I was confused, because he had invited me to his house to meet his friend. He said, "It doesn't seem like you are interested in Phil, so why don't we get it on?" I pulled away and headed back to the poolroom.

I looked around the house and wondered what it would be like to live there. Everything was top notch. I could live like this, I thought to myself. I was definitely attracted to his wealth. We played pool, visited, and before long, Peter was walking me through the house again as an excuse to get close to me. He suddenly took me in his arms and began kissing me. I was shocked at his boldness. He was 45, and I was 28—he held all the cards.

Peter turned out to be a sex addict and suffered from a well-masked low self-esteem. Three things drove him: his boys, aged four and one; sex; and money, reflected in all the big boys' "toys" money could buy. He was on a quest to prove to the world that he was a success. I was on a quest to apply love. We dated for six months.

One of my most terrifying moments with Peter came at his gorgeous lake home in the interior of beautiful British Columbia. He and I would go there together about once a month. I had by then discovered that he had a Jekyll and Hyde nature. On this particular occasion, we had been working on the cabin all day. At one point, he began to throw pot shots out at me. One minute he was nice, and the next minute he would call me a stupid bitch.

I responded by telling him to "grow up." He lost his composure and grabbed me. He sat me down in a wooden chair and started berating me. When I tried to get up, he threw me back down. He was six-foot-two and weighed about 200 pounds. I was scared, but I thought to myself: "Settle down—you need to get out of this alive." I began agreeing with him; I apologized for my stupidity, and thanked him for sharing his place.

I had come with him in his car, and I knew that he could potentially harm me, so I needed to be nice to him to have a chance to get home safely. I played it cool. We left the lake house that evening, and when we returned to Calgary, I went back to my own home, disconnected the phone, and created a plan to get out of the relationship—carefully.

In the following months, Peter simmered down, or perhaps I just got better at knowing how not to stir him. I slowly moved the romantic relationship into a friendship. Eventually, when he fell for another woman, I was able put that relationship behind me.

STUDYING AND APPLYING THE COURSE

I began to understand that for many individuals, the initial desire to integrate the lessons outlined in the Course created a perception of a tearing down, or a loss of what was once perceived as valuable. As a student and teacher of the Course, I have witnessed many of my study group students having that same perception. I, however, did not experience this when I began my journey—not because I was better than other students, but because, in my perception, I had already lost all that was truly valuable. My experience of the initial stages in working with the Course was uplifting and inspiring.

The more I read and learned, the more I remembered what Helen had taught me and what I had inherently remembered as a young child. For me, receiving *A Course in Miracles'* message of love and the deeper awareness of how the ego functions created a pathway home.

One evening, as I was meditating, the thought came, "I should teach this stuff to Eve." Then I thought, "No way; she is too 'fundamental,' too obsessed with the belief in punishment and hell, *but maybe someday.*"

I had been studying the Course via *A Return to Love* for approximately four months, when I was sitting at my dining room table one day. I said a prayer, and at that moment, I vowed to be a student and teacher of the Course for the rest of my life. I said to the Great Orchestrating Design that I would teach as many as I could the powerful message contained within that text. Then I made "a deal." I said that if I could get a job in which I could have more dollars per hour and benefits for the boys, I would give all the rest of my time over to teaching the Course. I then "upped" the ante one more notch by saying that if I were to find a man who offered financial freedom and would love my children, I would dedicate the rest of my days to the Course, and that one day I would build a center founded on the Course principles, and write a book helping students understand its simple message, "Only love is real, nothing else exists, and herein lies the peace of God."

Months following my agreement with God, I applied for a daytime bartender position at one of Calgary's best hotels. Starting wage was $8.25 per hour; all benefits were available, including an RRSP program if I wanted to invest in my future. When I was called in by the HR Department, I prayed and simply said, "Thy will be done, not mine."

I had a wonderful interview with Tessa, the Human Resources Manager, but weeks passed without a call from her. I trusted and continued to believe that God had a plan.

Eventually, in early June, Tessa did call. She said that the position for bartender had been filled internally, but that now there was a position for a fulltime day cocktail server, and she asked if I was interested. I accepted the job and began fulfilling my part of "the deal," which was to practice the Course principles with everyone I encountered.

I loved my job; every day I went in and thought of the lounge as my church. Each day, I had a different collection of dance partners; each person helping me to love all sides of myself.

CHAPTER 11

$\mathcal{H}$oly $\mathcal{E}$ncounters

It was the Remembrance Day weekend in November 1993, and I was scheduled to work the night shift, which started at 5 P.M. The boys were with Jake for the weekend, which meant some greatly appreciated playtime for me.

When I arrived at work that afternoon, I learned that it was the birthday of one of our colleagues. The rest of the lounge team was going to dinner, and then out for drinks at one of their favorite pubs to celebrate. I was asked to join them after my shift, which would normally end around 9 or 10 P.M. It seemed like a perfect arrangement as far as the timing was concerned.

The hotel was at about 30 percent occupancy, which meant I would be getting off early, and by 7 P.M., the night bartender sent me off to celebrate with the others. There was just one problem: I worked downtown, but lived in the far south of Calgary. I knew that I would probably not be able to go home and then get back downtown for the 9 P.M. meeting. I decided that I needed to kill some time until I could meet up with the others at the pub.

But what should I do in the meantime? I remembered Earls, a mingling bar that I had visited a few weeks earlier. I had gone there with a girlfriend and had quite enjoyed the atmosphere. This bar was known as one of the better places to go for meeting people.

I thought about checking it out for an hour or so, and then making my way to the pub to meet up with my friends. I took my time changing after my shift; I stalled as much as possible because I was beginning to feel inhibitions about going into the bar alone. When I finally arrived at Earls, I drove around, circling the bar, which has all glass windows in the front, so it was easy to see just how busy it was inside. I quickly began to lose confidence.

My inner voice was urging me to go inside. I was arguing with it, and was beginning to question why I thought it was so important for me to go in. My guidance then came up with a good and doable plan: "Go inside and look around as if you are supposed to meet someone," it suggested. "Then, if you don't see anyone you know, and you still feel uneasy, you can leave." Just try it, I thought, I am a bartender, and this is my normal working arena. I took heart, parked the car, and went inside.

ANGEL ENCOUNTER OF THE MOST MYSTERIOUS KIND

Immediately through the doors and sitting up at the bar was Judy from the hotel's sales office. She took one look at me, pointed to the seat next to her, and said, "Come sit." I told her that I had about an hour and a half to go until I could meet my friends for dinner, and she said, "Well, then you will just have to kill some time with the girls and me." "What a relief," I thought. "My inner voice was right again."

About 20 minutes into our visit, I looked across the bar and noticed a dark-haired guy pointing directly at me while speaking to another attractive man beside him. Our eyes locked. I could see that he felt embarrassed because I had caught him pointing at me, but then I smiled. He smiled back and carried on the conversation with his friend. A few minutes later, I felt someone tapping on my shoulder. It was that same dark-haired man whom I had looked at only moments earlier. He introduced himself as Allan; it was obvious that he had had a few drinks, which had increased his level of courage. His attractive friend stood beside him.

They were there to meet me, said Allan. "Oh, really?" I said, smiling, while I thought, now there's a pickup line I haven't heard before! With hand outstretched, his friend said, "Hi, I'm Dave." I shook his hand, and we all began telling jokes.

The hours flew by, and before we knew it, I was inviting Allan and Dave to tag along with me to the pub, to meet up with the rest of the birthday gang. Strangely, I felt as though I had known Dave and Allan forever. They agreed to follow me to the pub in their own cars.

After we arrived at the pub, I learned that Allan and Dave had just met that same evening. They had been introduced to each other by someone who had found out that both their mothers' name was Donna—a coincidence that prompted them to bond instantly.

Dave was a lawyer, a profession I had always considered pursuing, and Allan was the owner of a heavy truck dealership. "Peterbilt trucks," he said, "are the best you can buy—they are the Mercedes of trucks." His pride of ownership was evident to me, and I admitted to him that I loved big trucks, too.

I was enjoying the company of both men, and at the end of the evening, I gave them both my phone number. In my heart, I wanted Dave to call most of all.

It was almost 3 A.M. by the time I finally drove home. I was at an intersection close to my home, waiting at a red light, when, to my surprise, Allan pulled up in his charcoal-black Mercedes Benz. He rolled down the smoked glass window and smiled. I smiled back and continued homeward.

My last turn was a looping road that passed under the main roadway. I wondered why Allan was following me, but did not feel concerned about it. Eventually, he began flashing his lights at me. I pulled over, and he came to the window. "I am not following you," he said. "I made a mistake. When I saw you turn off onto this road, I thought that maybe you were pulling off to tell me something, so I followed. Then I realized you were just going home. I didn't want you to think I was stalking you, so I thought

I'd better pull you over to explain." I understood and suggested that he come up to my place for some coffee before continuing home, to which he agreed.

Allan told me that after I had left, Dave had given him my number and said, "You two are a perfect pair, a great couple. Call her and make it work!" Then Dave drove away, never to be seen again. We went back to that same bar for years to come, but no one had ever seen Dave before or since. We now refer to him as matchmaker Angel Dave!

A DINNER TO REMEMBER

At 10 A.M. the next morning, Allan called to ask if I still wanted to come out to see his acreage. I agreed, but wondered if we would still feel so at ease with each other. He later told me that he could not quite remember what I looked like, but was hoping that I would be as pretty as he remembered me to be from the night before. When he saw me get out of the car, he smiled, feeling relieved.

Allan's house was an old farmhouse that had been transformed into a modern-day home. He was proud as a peacock to show it off. He walked me through the house and then through his renovations album. He talked about his former girlfriend and how she was a city gal and hadn't felt comfortable in the country. I noticed from the way he spoke about her that he seemed to be over her completely. I was impressed, and relieved—this was not going to be another "Peter" story!

Allan asked me to go to town with him. He suggested that we would get a cappuccino and a muffin, and then pick up his farm cat from the vet. She had been spayed the day before. I had nothing better to do, so I went. After we had coffee, he took me to a country gift store that was all decked out for Christmas. He bought me a bag of pot-pourri with cinnamon and cloves. Wow! I thought, he is different from all the others!

As we walked through the store, he would place his hand gently on my back. I felt like pulling away; I didn't like it at all. Somehow when he got too close, I felt suffo-cated; I didn't understand why. He did it repeatedly. "This is not going to work!" I thought to myself.

Next, we picked up the cat. She had been raised in the wild before she came to live on Allan's farm. Not having been litter-trained, she had an "accident" in the car on the way home. I used some tissue to clean up the mess. The fact that Allan didn't flinch, even though the interior of his Mercedes had become soiled, shone out in my mind to be a marker of his deeper character; I was impressed.

After we had brought the cat back to the farm, Allan asked me to go to dinner with him. As we talked over a bottle of red wine in an Italian restaurant that evening, I could tell that he was quickly falling in love with me. I was conversing with my inner voice on what to do about the lack of chemical attraction I felt towards him. "This is never going to work," I said to my inner voice. "He is an awesome guy, but I can't date someone I'm not sexually attracted to." The inner voice was silent. Allan continued to make me laugh and was more openhearted than I had ever experienced a man to be.

We talked and talked about love, kids, my girls, about his love relationships, trucks, and on and on. He was perfect, so why didn't I want to make love to him? Even the thought of it made me recoil. "Allan is a great-looking man. Any woman would want him—what is wrong with me?" I thought.

Then, out of the blue, a strong inner voice—one I did not normally hear—spoke. "Just open your heart and see who he is." I turned my attention to my heart and looked Allan right in the eyes all the way to his soul. Instantly, it felt as if a magic switch had been turned on—I saw him not with my head, but with my heart. My soul knew his—I knew that we had shared a dance before, although I couldn't remember which one, or when. I just knew that if I wanted to, I could dance with him again. And suddenly I wanted to.

When we got back to my house, Allan told me he did not feel confident about driving home after so much red wine. I agreed and suggested he could spend the night at my place. He said that we would "just cuddle." He had much more in mind.

We tucked ourselves into bed, and I began reading to him from *A Return to Love*. The fact that I was reading the principles of *A Course in Miracles* to him on our first evening together and showing him my passion for spiritual values in a relationship, set the stage for the direction our relationship would take. My intention was that it would move from a *Special Relationship*, which is how all relationships start out, into a *Holy Relationship*, meaning that we would both be whole and wanting to share that wholeness with each other. However, Allan was not listening to me read that night; he was too busy admiring my negligee.

THE FEAR OF LETTING GO

Three weeks after Allan and I consummated our relationship, he broke out in a head-to-toe rash. He looked like he was the victim of a burn accident. His condition was ugly and painful. He was diagnosed with the worst case of psoriasis his doctor had ever seen. We were stumped; why did this happen? Why just after he met me? Did I have something to do with it? Did having an instant family have something to do with it? Did the fact that he usually was a "totally-in-control kind of guy who was going to find himself out of control" have something to do with it? Was this his ego's way of trying to get us apart? Yes, to all of these.

One of the most memorable sets of words that Allan ever wrote to me in a card was, "My spirit adores you, but my ego isn't quite so fond of you." This was the thought pattern behind the psoriasis, and in the next six years, the battle between his spirit and his ego was reflected in the severity of his skin irritation.

OUR DANCE

Allan and I dated, or rather practically lived together, for the first six months. Then the hotel where I worked offered its employees an excellent deal. They had recently purchased a resort in Cuba and were offering exceptional packages to employees. In May of 1994, Allan and I went on our trip. We spent an awesome week together. Then, on our last night before returning home, I pitched the big question over dinner. I asked him if I should renew my lease on the condo I was renting. The lease was up June 1.

He asked how I felt about moving in with him, and I answered that it was the natural next step, since we had only been apart a couple of nights since our magical first dinner. He asked if I would quit my job, and work on the acreage instead. He said he would provide me with a monthly income to cover all the family needs. I agreed, and resigned from my job at the hotel a week later.

When something small and meaningless happens,
it is protecting something big that is being born.

Caroline Myss

CHAPTER 12

Sometimes Love Means Saying Goodbye

Allan and I were like husband and wife from the start. Jeremy and Joe fell in love with him as much as I did. Allan loved being a stepparent. He was hoping that the boys would call him "Dad," but Jake made it clear that he would be hurt if they did.

Even though my son Joe loved Allan, he still secretly hoped that one day, his dad and I would reconcile. The alternate weekends when the boys were with their father were both wonderful and heart-wrenching. They were wonderful because Allan and I had time alone as a couple. But they were heart-wrenching because, with the boys away, I missed my girls even more.

Allan was becoming increasingly concerned about the way Adam and Eve ran my life. He sensed that his presence seemed to create a distance between the girls and me. We concluded that Adam and Eve were feeling threatened by Allan's wealth. I had long since become desensitized to their incessant need to control and was well able to overlook most of their continued hurtful actions and words.

By August 1994, Emma was turning thirteen. One day, she announced to everyone's surprise that she would be moving in with us. I had always said to the girls that, at any time and under any condition, I would take them back if they wanted to come and live with us. Emma took us up on the open-ended offer. Adam and Eve were furious, and I knew that things were going to get ugly as a result of Emma's decision.

Eve called. I could tell by her voice that she definitely was "a woman scorned." She asked if we had, in fact, agreed to Emma's moving in with us. I said that yes, this was fine with Allan and me. Eve and Adam dropped Emma off the next day.

Emma came to me packing a whole lot of rage because her life had been so controlled by Adam and Eve, and five garbage bags full of physical belongings that had been thrown together as a way of sending a message—"You have betrayed us, and so now go!" Emma knew in her heart that it had always been a choice of one house or the other. The choice she had just made came with a considerable price tag, in particular the severed relationship with her siblings. At that particular time, it was a price she was willing to pay.

The next day, Emma called Tasha to see how things were. Tasha told her that Adam and Eve had moved her into

Emma's room the same day Emma had moved out. Emma asked if Tasha was going to continue coming on weekends. Tasha said no; Sara had not come for months already.

The first month together with Emma was wonderful. I could hardly believe that after all these years, she was back in my arms and back in my life. I was determined to prove to her that I was a great mom. Then, after the second month, Emma began to show her other side more and more frequently. She was rude, cruel with her words, and unkind to her brothers Joe and Jeremy. Soon everyone in the house began to tiptoe so as not to upset her. She was lying, smoking, drinking, and, yes, being a teen. I had no idea how to please her, and I became terrified of getting her angry and seeing her leave again. She had me right where she wanted me.

By the beginning of month five, I was burning out. Emma had refused to phone or visit Adam and Eve or her siblings. Eve would show up at Emma's school, telling the teachers stories about how I was forbidding contact between the homes. Emma was becoming more and more unreasonable, and unmanageable. Then, one day, while she was throwing one of her usual dirty looks at me, Allan snapped.

He told her it was enough, that he was no longer going to allow a thirteen-year-old to run his house. He said he was appalled at the way she treated me after all the heartbreak he had watched me endure. He said he was fed up with the way she treated her little brothers—bossing them around all the time. Finally, he told her that she would need to change her behavior, or he would take her back to Adam and Eve's house. She heard him, she changed, and I thought things were going to be fine.

*No problem can be solved from
the same consciousness that created it.
We must learn to see the world anew.*

Albert Einstein

CHAPTER 13

Judgment Day

In December, Emma finally heeded my urgings to call her other home. Christmas was coming, and she was beginning to miss her sisters and her brother Luke—Adam and Eve's son. She called, and realized that they missed her and wanted her to visit. She said she would think about it. By Christmas, she had made a few calls to them. We had shopped for presents for Tasha, Sara, and Luke, and Emma wondered if I thought it would be okay for her to go on a weekend visit. I assured her that it would be fine, and that we could start to mend feelings slowly.

Emma left on the first weekend of January 1995. She was to be returned at 6 P.M. on Sunday, but did not come home. At seven, I called their house. Adam answered the phone. I asked where Emma was, to which he sarcastically replied, "Here." I asked why she was late. "According to whom?" he answered. "According to Emma," I answered, "and the years of court order time frames." When the girls had come to visit me, I had always taken them home by six on Sunday; in fact, the kids had become terrified if I was late returning them.

Adam told me they were watching a movie, and that he would bring Emma back by 8:30. I agreed. Then Emma came on the phone and asked me if she could bring home a parakeet. I said not that night, but that we would all talk about it as a family, and decide together. "I knew you would say that," she answered, "Mom and Dad said you would say that, too." I knew that things were bad when she said that. In Adam and Eve's home, much of the weekend had been spent talking about comparing households, and they had determined that they had more to offer.

At 8:45 they arrived, all of them—Adam, Eve, Tasha, Emma, and Luke. Eve got out of the van. By then, Allan was extremely frustrated about their childish behavior. He came out of the house with his voice raised, telling them that solutions needed to be found. Eve began screaming at him about his being one of a long lineup of guys I had gone through. He told her to shut up and said that she and Adam needed to act like adults when moving kids between homes. Adam yelled out, "There won't be any more moves between homes!" He said that Emma would be staying with them.

I remained calm and collected; I knew that force was not going to work with Adam and Eve. I walked towards the van and asked Emma to come into the house with me.

Eve locked the van door and told her to stay in the van. All the children were hysterical and yelling at me—telling me that they never wanted to see me again. For ten minutes, I calmly pleaded with Emma to just come into the house with me. She did nothing—her eyes said, "I want to come," while her actions said, "I can't."

Eve was filled with rage, pushing me, and telling me that it was too late—Emma was staying with them. Adam stayed by the van, yelling over the roof. I sent Allan inside, telling him this was not the way to deal with things; he flew up his hands and went into the house. There was a lot of swearing; the incident reminded me of my childhood days, when I would watch my parents go into similar fits of rage. Eve was just like my mother—a grandstander. The last thing you do with them is play into their drama. I knew this, but Allan didn't. Eventually, they drove away. In my heart, I knew that Emma was gone, again.

A couple of hours later, I called their house to speak with Emma. I wanted to go and pick her up. Adam answered, and he told me that he would make sure I never saw or spoke with the children again.

I called Emma the next day while Adam was at work, and I told her I would do anything to get her back if she wanted to live with me. She said no; she and Tasha asked me to get out of their lives and leave them alone.

I called again a few days later; they said the same thing over again. My heart bled with pain. I asked Emma if she wanted me to pack up her room and return her belongings; she said yes. I complied and surrendered again. Packing up her room for a second time was unbearable.

Allan was glad she was gone, and so were the boys. No one missed her but I.

I prayed for guidance; my inner voice answered, "You could teach Eve what you know about love. You could help her see that the past is overlooked by love." "No way, get someone else to help her, I will pray for her and no more," was my response.

A week after the incident in the driveway, the local police department called. Eve had filed aggravated assault charges against Allan, and we were asked to go to the police station and write out a statement that would later become evidence to be used in court.

We did what they asked and hired a lawyer. The statements that were entering into evidence had been written by Adam and Eve and all four children. No two stories matched up—they couldn't, because the event had never occurred. The police officer said that when there is such a dramatic discrepancy between statements, a trial date is automatically set.

Allan was mortified; he regularly traveled to the USA on business, and if he would, in fact, be found guilty of aggravated assault, he would have a criminal record and be forbidden to enter other countries.

After Emma had left, I had thought about all the perceived injustice I had encountered through Adam and Eve; I had spent hours thinking about it, and I just couldn't stand by and do nothing. I asked Allan if he would support me in fighting to get Emma back; he said no. "And if you fight for that, you will have to go," he said as he pointed to the door.

I plummeted into a quiet despair, unable to discuss my feelings with anyone. A few days later, I vigilantly turned back to the Course principles. Allan was both angry and frustrated with the alleged charges laid against him, and we began to grow apart.

Soul Contracts

It was Allan's 42nd birthday, and I decided to get several of his managers together to celebrate at a nearby pub. I was looking around the crowd, when I spotted Lance. He and I had met while I worked in the lobby lounge of a downtown hotel the previous year. When we recognized each other, we both lit up, just as we had on that earlier occasion. We were delighted to see each other and began chatting about all of the events that had transpired in our lives.

At the time of that first meeting with Lance, as he walked into the lounge, my inner voice said: "See who he is." I did not understand the comment then, and would not until several months into the future. In the days after our meeting, we would chat about everything from how the universe works to his love life. I was not initially attracted to him physically, but did notice that he resembled my dad when he was Lance's age. Lance was 32 when we met.

What really drew me towards him was that he shared an interest in spiritual matters and in the exploration of the mind and how it worked. When I told him I would be retiring from the hotel industry because I would be working on Allan's farm, he became sad because he wouldn't see me at the hotel anymore, but glad for me and my new-found love with Allan.

On the occasion of Allan's birthday celebration, Lance and I were brought together once again, and I realized how I hungered to share my spiritual wisdom with a friend. We chatted for a while, exchanged phone numbers, and decided that we would get together for lunch sometime.

A month passed, and I was delving deeper and deeper into the Course. My spiritual search was driving Allan crazy, but it was lifting me out of the depression I felt as a result of Emma's moving out.

I was beginning to see things through a new set of eyes. I was again filled with joy and faith in the Great Orchestrating Design. But at the same time, Allan was wanting less and less to do with my spirituality.

One day, as I was cleaning up, the phone rang. When I answered, a warm, familiar voice said, "Hello, it's Lance. How are you?" I was so glad to hear from him, and we chatted for a while, catching up on the most recent changes in our lives. We agreed to meet for lunch the following week. During that meeting, as well as a subsequent one, we talked about many things, but mostly he was fascinated by my knowledge of the principles in *A Course in Miracles* and how to apply them. Since he loved to talk about spirituality as much as I did, we were growing closer as spiritual friends, while Allan and I were growing farther apart as life partners.

A few weeks later, Lance and I began to meet regularly to visit his dying father, who was ill and suffering in the last stages of Alzheimer's. Through hours and hours of discussion, I discovered that Lance and I had lots in common from our similar childhoods. Our shared wounds worked as a bridge to my heart. I cared about Lance deeply and was willing to do anything to help him look after his dad, or to lighten his burdens.

I never thought seriously about a romantic relationship with Lance until one day, he gave me a cassette tape that he had made. I was quite surprised by his choice of songs, which were filled with both spiritual lyrics and romance. He invited me to accompany him to a Calgary Flames hockey game, and I went, even though Allan didn't want me to go. Allan intuitively picked up on Lance's private agenda for the direction of the relationship with me.

Initially, I brushed off the subtle romantic invitation I perceived from Lance. I decided that, since we had never crossed any such line, I was misunderstanding the choice of songs on the cassette. I could not believe that Lance had more than friendship in mind, because I had been so open and upfront about my relationship with Allan.

One day, however, I asked Lance if he was romantically attracted to me, and, sheepishly, he said yes. I told him that, although Allan and I were having tough times in our relationship, I was not ready to leave it, and Lance understood.

A few more weeks passed, and things became increasingly hostile between Allan and me. I had become resigned to the fact that our relationship was never going to work because he so resisted my spirituality. The idea of leaving the relationship was becoming a reality faster than either Allan or I realized.

For the next two weeks, I cried and grieved for Allan's and my lost love. Allan seemed unfeeling and unimpressed with my wailing, but he did not realize that with every tear I shed, I was getting closer to leaving the relationship.

Dad, Lance, and I

On January 1, 1995, a few days after Emma left, I received a telephone voice-message from my father. I had not heard from him in over twelve years. I had prayed for the healing of our relationship and had turned it over to the Holy Spirit's care. My feelings about his call were mixed. I wondered whether, if we reestablished our relationship, he would abandon me once again, as he had done when I was only seven.

I prayed about the situation, and returned his call. Soon we began catching up. He seemed unnaturally receptive to the idea of healing our bruised relationship. Later, I learned that it was his common-law wife who was behind his attempt at reconciliation.

Regardless of whose idea it was, I was delighted, because I so wanted to have a better understanding of his perspective on my earlier childhood years. Mom had told so many stories—it was hard to know what was truth, and what was fantasy and lies.

Dad shared with me that he had befriended a woman named Adele, who had wanted to meet his children and grandchildren. He said Adele had been pushing for a reunited family, and so he thought he would give it a try.

A few weeks later, Dad, Adele, Allan, and I went to dinner. It was a great experience, and the beginning of my pathway back into my family heritage. We visited often until late into the night when he was on a stopover in the city.

A few months later, Dad suggested an Easter family vacation at his part-time home in Florida, and Allan and I agreed to go with the boys. But a few days before our scheduled departure, I told Allan that, in light of all the coolness between us, I felt that we needed a break from each other and that I would go to Florida with the boys and leave him at home to think the situation over. He was agreeable and undisturbed by the idea at first, but then, with each subsequent passing day, he began to fall apart. The day I left for the airport was heart-wrenching; I left feeling that his heart was broken, and so was mine.

While in Florida, I spent time reflecting on the relationship as a whole, and realized that it was based on lack. It was a *Special Relationship* sustained by "hidden agendas," as all relationships are. It became clear that our longtime survival as life partners was dependent upon our having an open, honest relationship with each other and with God. Since Allan openly declared that he was not interested in that, it became obvious that I should leave the relationship. I decided that, on my return, I would find a place of my own, and move out.

Lance and I hadn't spoken to each other since the night of the hockey game. One day, while in Florida, I began to feel anxious about his father and decided to give Lance a call to see how his dad was doing. Lance told me he didn't feel that his father had much time left. I listened and tried to console him. I shared with him that I would be leaving my relationship with Allan, and that I was not sure how things would end up. In my heart, I began to wonder if I should pursue a relationship with Lance, since we shared such a deep interest in spirituality.

The news of my impending breakup with Allan shocked Lance. He seemed distant and confused. It was apparent that I had taken him by surprise. I knew that the primary drawing card Lance had was that he loved my spirituality, while Allan hated it. I wondered if Lance knew this as well as I did.

I was going through some profound spiritual changes during this period, and all my psychic abilities were blown open. I was writing poetry, seeing auras around people, and having many telepathic experiences. I didn't fully understand what was happening to me, so I went to see a well-respected psychic while in Florida. She confirmed most of what I wanted to hear, namely that Lance was now the supporter of my spiritual path and Allan was obstructing it. I took this information as a confirmation that I should leave Allan. In addition, the psychic's message was congruent with the guidance I heard within, and the deepened yearning I was feeling to be with Lance.

The psychic also saw me write many books, and work with a "special gift," which was then reawakening. She spoke at length about the hard times in the past, but also about my resilient nature. She concluded our session by saying that I was in a phase of deep spiritual healing.

When I returned from Florida, a quick series of coincidences occurred that allowed me to move out of Allan's house within a week following my return. Moving-out day was unbelievably hard on Allan; he was trying to do and say anything he could to make me change my mind.

I had come to the conclusion that Allan and I had become addicted to each other. We had discussed this at length, and I realized that, as with any addiction, we felt good only when we were getting our "hit," thus feeling in control. Since all addiction will eventually take us back to God, the sobering up and deprival of the "substance," in whichever form it comes, leaves us feeling terrified and powerless. On the other hand, the reestablishing of our relationship to self or God imparts a deeply nurturing and satisfying authentic inner power. At the time, I was further down that path than was Allan.

I had shed my tears for the relationship and had become cool and uninterested in Allan's requests for "another chance." My inner guidance told me repeatedly that I was to get out of the way, and that the Great Orchestrating Design had a plan that involved my being unavailable to him. I trusted that guidance above all else. I had made the decision that if Allan decided to establish a relationship with God for himself and not only for me, I would consider the possibility of recommitting to the relationship.

In the weeks that followed, I did a lot of soul-searching. I became sexually intimate with Lance, but in my heart I knew that what I truly needed was a long-term partner and stepfather for my sons—a role that Lance was not prepared to take on. I knew that we had very deep-running feelings for each other, but that this was not enough to sustain a relationship. Soon he stopped returning my calls; I knew our dance was over. I grieved for someone to share my soul with—someone who would pursue God with me; someone who loved the things I loved.

Once again, I felt confused and abandoned, as I had felt

with other men. It felt as I had as a child, when I realized Dad was not going to be back. I realized in that moment that Lance was helping me to get over the belief that if I was not good enough, men would leave me.

I don't imagine that Lance ever really knew why he played this part in my life, but I do, and for that I am truly grateful.

HOLY LOVE

Allan and I had lived apart for exactly two months when I saw him one day at one of my sons' soccer games, which Allan had continued to attend because he had become so connected with the children. He said, "I want to thank you for helping me." I looked puzzled and he said, "I found God, and I now know how important it is to know God, individually." He had changed, and so had I. I silently wondered if we could begin again.

I had stopped talking to Lance a month earlier. At the time, I was fully prepared to continue my journey on my own and without any man, although, in my heart, I hoped for a *Holy Relationship* with Allan. I was meditating one summer day, when I heard my inner voice say, "You can go 'home' now; call Allan." I did so reluctantly, because I knew how upset Allan was that I had become involved with Lance. He felt betrayed. I understood, yet I also knew in my heart the greater purpose for Lance's interlude in our lives. I asked Allan to go for lunch with me, and he hesitantly agreed. He told me that he was not sure he was willing to give our relationship another try, or whether I would be able to recommit to the relationship. He felt bitter towards Lance for getting involved with me when he knew that I was in a common-law relationship with Allan. But slowly, Allan worked through all his deep feelings of betrayal, day by day, and step by step. I repeatedly explained to him that, since spirituality was my top value, I felt closer to those who supported it and felt distanced by those who didn't. Eventually he, too, realized that I was committed not to a person, but to my highest value—pursuing God. Over the following months, Allan grew in his understanding of this truth, and in March 1996, we were married.

Reflections on the Dance

Many individuals have become confused about the deeply moving emotions that sometimes arise between souls. The common belief is that these electric, insatiable, and intoxicating feelings identify that we have found our long sought-after soulmate. I believed this initially as well, but have since realized that intense sexual energy is reflective of shared core wounds, rather than a deeper soul love.

Lance and I had both had volatile childhood relationships with our parents. We had each parented our parents, as both his parents and my father had been alcohol abusers. We had both perceived that we were never good enough for our fathers. And both Lance and I were searching for love in external relationships, rather than internally within our own beings. Therefore, I have since come to realize that the real reason for the overpowering feelings that ensued between us was reflective of two souls that were interacting through shared wounds. Often, these are perceived to be identical. The electricity is an animated field that supports the revealing and healing of the soul's unloved memories and wounds. When either person, or both, sees the truth of these unloved memories, the feelings between them subside and vanish. Special Love is then transformed into holy, unpossessive feelings of gratitude and love.

An in-depth look at the authentic "soulmate" relationship can be found in the last chapter of Part 2.

MENDING HEARTS – REBUILDING TRUST

Many of us will experience what we perceive is a betrayal by someone in our life. The deepest wounds occur when we have placed our expectations on a loved one, which means that we have imposed our particular values upon them. Ultimately, they either can't or won't live up to them, and we experience that as betrayal.

Allan, for instance, is very monogamous in his romantic values. I, on the other hand, am open-minded in the understanding that an individual can be intimately connected in many ways to many people. I know, however, that if I want to sustain my relationship with Allan, I must practice fidelity. Since, in Allan's perception, I had gone against his value of fidelity, he needed to expand his understanding. Originally, he had believed that if any woman had practiced acts of infidelity, he would no longer be able to trust and love her, but since I challenged that belief, he discovered that his love was stronger than this particular value of his.

My part in the healing of his heart was to speak openly and honestly about all the feelings and reasons I believed that this incident had happened. It took both of us to create the situation and both of us to heal it. Consequently, I was willing to answer all his questions when he asked them from a place of insecurity, not when he was charged with anger.

Commonly, when an act of infidelity has occurred, there is a surge of imaginings that go on in the non-participating partner. I spent time assuring Allan that it was not a quest for sex that drove this act, but a quest for self-worth and validation. Once he saw this clearly, the competitive feelings eased. With time, they passed completely. Most of us want to be "the One," but this is an illusory desire. Each of us is "the One" only as long as we are meeting our partner's needs better than the next person.

Each of us is on a quest to becoming fully human, fully actualized, and love-encompassing. Each individual's experiences arise so that they can learn how to love all situations, and all parts of themselves. This is necessary in the ever-expansive journey called love. The journey is detoured each time we become overrun with guilt, shame, blame, or dishonesty.

If a couple doesn't work consciously on rebuilding trust, then the relationship will be extinguished by fear.

THE ASSAULT TRIAL

Almost a year had passed before we went to trial in the assault charges against Allan, and I had not seen or spoken to the children since the alleged incident. We had asked for a plea bargain several times in order to spare the children from going to court. We knew it was all a lie, and we did not want the children to be cross-examined and found caught up in lies. Each time, our offer was denied.

On the morning of the trial, Emma, Tasha, Adam, and Eve were there. The crown prosecutor pulled our attorney aside and asked for a plea bargain. She said that she had met with Eve earlier and felt that she was both emotionally and psychologically unstable. We accepted the offer to have a peace bond put in place, which meant that Allan was not permitted to knowingly be within a two-kilometre proximity of Eve.

CHAPTER 14

ℱor ℒove or ℳoney

Eighteen long months passed before I worked up the courage to call the girls to see if I could have a dinner visit with them. I was overjoyed when my request was granted. During the visit, many questions about our situation and the previous years were asked and answered. I felt that the visit was successful and that it offered hope for building a better relationship between the girls and me. Apparently, the visit was perceived in a positive light by the girls as well, because Adam and Eve subsequently became very threatened by the possibility of our having a healed relationship, and they denied me all further access to the girls.

I prayed for direction and an answer; my inner voice replied, "Write Eve a letter and teach her that love transcends fear, teach her the Course principles, teach her that the past does not have to run the present or future." I refused, "Get someone else to teach her; I can't believe you want me, of all people, to help her—no way!"

A few months later, I hired a lawyer and began legal proceedings to enforce the visitation right that I had been awarded ten years earlier. The request was received at the court, and an order was issued to uphold the interim access until the trial. We made a request for an assessment of the family dynamics; it, too, was granted.

Shortly thereafter, we received a request for our financial records from Adam and Eve's attorney—they were suing for child support, requesting $600 per child a month. In addition, they were requesting the court to take away all previously awarded visitation and custody rights.

The first issue for me to attend to was to have an independent assessment done to prove that the girls suffered from Parent Alienation Syndrome. When this syndrome occurs, the children believe that they are "freethinking," although they are not. It is a form of brainwashing.

Over time, a parent or caregiver will send out clues, both subtle and obvious, that they do not approve of the other parent. In the most hostile extreme, the caregiving parent will threaten the child should they request visitation of the alienated parent. The children in this situation begin to learn that life is easier if they go along with the alienation. In extreme cases, the child or the children will respond as though the alienated parent had harmed them.

Parent Alienation Syndrome can also negatively affect the parent-grandparent relationship. If this is suspected, I would advise immediate professional intervention. Usually, children affected by this syndrome eventually come to understand that they have been psychologically swayed against the parent. Individuals who are probable to enter into the dynamics of Parent Alienation Syndrome are those who suffer from a deep sense of insecurity. They are often overly controlling, and intimidating by nature.

Allan and I went to see Karen, a well-respected professional specializing in Parent Alienation Syndrome. She listened to our concerns and then met with Adam and Eve.

She later reported that she believed our situation to be an extreme case of this syndrome, but felt that with the age of the children—Emma (15), Tasha (14), and Sara (12)—the relationship was reparable, with appropriate counselling.

It was October, the month of Tasha's birthday, and I wanted her to have a gift from me. I gave Karen a purse with a note, earrings, and $40, to give to Tasha. The note reminded her that, no matter what, I loved her. I wasn't sure what things she liked, and so I thought some money would allow her to buy what she wanted. In the note, I also told her that anytime she wanted to call, she could.

Adam and Eve refused to continue seeing Karen, and the children refused to go as well. My lawyer and I discussed the issue and conceded that, even with the court order, given the girls' ages, they could not be forced to "listen" to the therapist. We surrendered and awaited the child support hearing.

I prayed that night, and asked for guidance. My inner voice directed me to write a letter explaining the Course principles. I refused, replying, "She is never going to listen to me; get someone else to teach her."

Affidavits moved frequently between the two sides. Adam and Eve's lawyer, Mick, was requesting financial income statements and previous tax reports for Allan. My attorney, Philip, denied the request based on the fact that Allan had no financial responsibility to the girls.

Philip was a well-seasoned family lawyer; he knew the laws pertaining to support and was almost certain that Allan's income would have no bearing on the requested child support payments. As it turned out, he was right!

We were preparing to enter the courtroom, when Mick walked over. He handed me the purse I had bought for Tasha. I felt sick, and when I looked inside, everything I had put there was still in it. Mick said that Tasha thought of it as a bribe. He suddenly seemed to realize just how hurtful it was for me, having to take it back. I walked into the courtroom with my heart broken, and feeling abandoned.

I sat alone on my side of the courtroom; Adam and Eve sat with a cheering crowd as usual. I was a seasoned courtroom listener; I prayed, "May thy will be done."

First, Mick presented his case to the judge, who was an attractive, well-polished woman. I sensed an inner wisdom from her and humble self-appreciation. I hoped that her gender would be in my favor. I had no idea if she had children of her own, or if she could relate to what really was at the root of Adam and Eve's request.

Mick was busy flinging out untruths and was apparently quite charged up about our refusal to submit exact income figures. We did disclose, however, that Allan's income exceeded $100,000 per year, which seemed to aggravate him even further. Mick tried every approach to convince the judge that Allan's income had to be considered in their request for $1,800 a month child support, arrears payment of a year, plus all legal fees.

The judge listened, no sign of which way she was swaying, although she did tell Mick flat out that Allan's income had no bearing in this case. He attempted a rebuttal; she hushed him, and sternly told him his request was ludicrous.

Philip approached, and told my story. The judge showed no emotion; she repeatedly looked me in the eye. She asked what my income was; Philip told her that it was $600 per month, from child support from the father of my two sons. This monthly income was not reliable because my former husband often missed payments and was several thousand dollars in arrears.

The judge asked Philip about the relationship I had with my second husband, the father of my sons. He told her it was a good relationship, without access problems of any kind. He mentioned that, although the boys' father was in arrears in child support payments, I never hindered the relationship between my sons and their father. Next, the judge asked if Allan had any children. Philip replied no, but said that he definitely believed that Allan had assumed the role of father to my two sons. He explained that Allan's level of commitment was in fact so great that, as part of the divorce agreement between Jake and me, he had legally assumed full financial responsibility for the boys.

Next, the judge asked why I did not currently work outside the home. Philip told her that I had been a working single mother for most of the time since my sons' births, but that now, as a stay-at-home mom, I volunteered at the school an average of three days a week. He continued by stating that Allan and I owned a large acreage, and that I cared for that also. He added that I was planning to go back to school and pursue a degree in psychology the following year.

The unusual thing about their conversation was that they talked about me as if I weren't there. I got a clear feeling that the judge was busy assessing my character. When she asked me to rise and to tell her why I wanted to be a psychologist, I replied that I loved people and I loved understanding how the mind works. I told her that I studied spirituality and loved to counsel. She replied, "Your life experience would have had something to do with your desire, I am sure." I did not reply, but she said, "Thank you; you may sit down."

Next, she said she needed a 15-minute break, after which she would give us the verdict. When she returned, she said that she had investigated whether or not she could deny the request for child support completely. She said that Alberta law required all parents to make a minimum payment of $100 per child to the day-to-day caregiver.

She said she was appalled by this couple's request, and denied them costs. She said that since they had already destroyed the relationship between the girls and their mother, there was no point in securing visitation access. She looked at me caringly and said, "I am sorry for what they have done. My prayer is that the monthly support payment of $300 until they each reach the age of 18 will show them in some fashion that you contributed to their life." She said that she was required by law to order a minimum of six months' arrears payments, and that I would have to pay those also. Next, she addressed the application by Adam and Eve that my request for legal custody be removed from the records. She denied that request, hoping that the girls would one day understand that the court had clearly seen the Parent Alienation that had occurred, and did not want to support Adam and Eve's decision to remove me from the girls' lives. The judge told me, "They will always be your children in your heart. I hope that one day, your girls will see what has happened here."

I sat breathlessly—she felt that she had done all she could to help enforce justice. I felt once again betrayed by the system.

Reflections on the Dance

As I reviewed this period of my life, I realized that since that time, I have helped so many understand the justice system and family law. Strangely enough, I often have clients that are going through similar experiences. Often, because of my experience, I can help prepare them for the journey.

Most recently, I have been dealing with fathers who are walking in moccasins similar to the ones I once wore. During the past two years, I helped a client and friend who never married his former partner gain custody and full-time care and control of his four-year-old daughter. This case is part of a small fraction of cases beginning to set a new precedent for unwed fathers to have full parental rights and to gain full custody of their children, even if they'd only had a brief relationship with the mother.

Was it worth my journey being able to help others? Absolutely.

CHAPTER 15

A Tiny Boxed Treasure

It was September of the following year. Allan and I were preparing to make our annual trip to the Truck Dealer Meeting. During the previous eleven months, I had been making support payments and had delved more and more deeply into my spiritual practice. Each time I went over another life hurdle, I plummeted deeper into the practice of the Course. I studied Deepak Chopra's work, dabbled in quantum physics, read books on Eastern Mysticism and Judaism, and explored anything else in which I could see similarities to the Course principles.

The Truck Dealer Meeting that year would begin a chain of events that truly revealed the awesome ways in which the Great Orchestrating Design is always maximizing our growth. As with all the "couple" dealer meetings, which alternate with the "stag" meetings every other year, spouses received a special gift of appreciation on the night of the awards dinner gathering. When we returned to our rooms, there would be a beautifully wrapped gift. This year was no exception. I opened the package, expecting a piece of high-priced crystal, similar to what I had received in previous years. This time, however, the gift turned out to be a tiny, light-yellow treasure chest with gold trim. It had hand-painted flowers on it; it was very sweet. I opened it and saw that it had a clean, white, polished surface. I wondered what I should put inside. I turned it over to see the name of the manufacturer. I was stunned—it was the same last name as Adam's.

I wondered about the oxymoron—a treasure chest with that name—where was the treasure in that? Oh well, grateful to have received anything at all, I packed it up and took it home.

A week later, I was at home, cleaning the house. I was listening to Barbra Streisand's CD *Higher Ground* (I would often play music that kept me focused on my spirit), when all the yearning in my heart to hold my girls rushed to the forefront of my being. I collapsed onto my knees, sobbing despairingly, and asked the heavens, "Why?"

Why did I have to be apart from them? What had I done in this or any other lifetime to be punished this way? What was I to learn? Why was I not getting the lesson? How much longer would it take me to understand the larger meaning of this plan? Why, when I practiced the principles of love, did I not get what I wanted? I begged for understanding; I begged for an answer.

My inner voice replied, "Have you ever considered that everything is in order—that each of you has come to learn specific lessons about themselves? Have you considered that you would never have pursued God so diligently without all these 'dances'? Do you realize that you would not have had your sons were it not for this experience? Do you realize your girls have agreed to this experience as souls searching to understand love also? My child, your life is now, and always has been, in order. This is not a punishment; it is a divine opportunity to learn what you came for–to learn about love's power, a mother's love, and the power of surrendering your limited understanding." Then the request came again, "Write Eve and teach her the Course principles." I finally surrendered to the request, repeatedly received. I was finally ready to do anything required to complete my soul contract.

I took pen to paper and wrote all morning–the letter I wrote was 13 pages long. It was filled with promises of a new beginning for us all, filled with hope, faith, and conviction in the power of love. I said that if we wanted, we could "let go of the past." If they were willing to start over, I was, too.

I shared the experience of my moccasins and validated theirs. I referred to one of Jesus' primary lessons, *to love thy neighbor as thyself.* I invited Eve to act, not just talk about, His teachings.

I told no one what I had done. I kissed the envelope, popped in a *Higher Ground* CD, suggested Eve purchase *A Return to Love,* and invited her to "dance." I stood at the mailbox and again said, "Thy will be done." I went home and released the outcome.

Three weeks passed by, my car was full of garlands and Christmas lights for the trees outside; I was preparing to "deck the halls." In my mind, I had finally done what the Holy Spirit had requested—I had written the letter and offered Eve a chance to start over.

I had not written the letter to get the girls back—I had written it to complete whatever contracts Eve's and my soul had. I practiced the Course teachings in that the only thing the children of God deserved was our gratitude and love, and I gave Eve both.

She sent back an 18-page letter. I devoured her every word, searching for confirmation that she was, in fact, willing to begin again. With that letter, I found a door opening to the possibility that we could finally heal our tattered relationship.

Following my repeated reading of the letter, I turned to the Course and asked the Holy Spirit for guidance. As I had done countless times before, I just opened the text to whatever page the Holy Spirit wanted me to read. My eyes fell upon the following passage:

> "You *are* your brother's savior. He is yours. Reason speaks happily indeed of this. This gracious plan was given love by Love. And what Love plans is like Itself in this: Being united, It would have you learn what you must be. And being one with It, it must be given you to give what It has given, and gives still. Spend but an instant in the glad acceptance of what is given you to give your brother, and learn with him what has been given both of you. To give is no more blessed than to receive. But neither is it less.
>
> The Son of God is always blessed as one. And as his gratitude goes out to you who blessed him,

reason will tell you that it cannot be you stand apart from blessing. The gratitude he offers you reminds you of the thanks your Father gives you for completing Him. And here alone does reason tell that you can understand what you must be. Your Father is as close to you as is your brother. Yet what is there that could be nearer you than is your Self?"

When Allan came home that evening, I told him, with tears rolling down my face, what I had done. He cried, too, and urged me to go slowly and carefully. I promised I would.

The next morning, I wrote Eve another letter. Later, as I ran downstairs to change the laundry from the washer to the dryer, I spotted the little treasure chest sitting on the entertainment centre. There was a single stream of sunlight shining right on it. I walked over with my heart in my throat, I got it—the message from heaven had been that there was a treasure in the name and in the right question. The question is, "Is there anything love will not heal?" In that moment, I knew with every cell of my being—and have never forgotten since—that the answer is *NO*.

*You can only lead others
where you yourself are willing to go.*

Lachlan Mclean

CHAPTER 16

A Second Life

A SECOND CHANCE

Eve and I wrote back and forth for a while, and eventually, the girls began writing, too. Tasha was initially the most interested in resuming a relationship. She was quick to acknowledge that the only way I could get to her and her sisters was through Eve.

About a month after my letter of invitation to heal and start over, Eve and I went for lunch together. The event was somewhat like our long meeting 14 years earlier at the Boston Pizza in Lethbridge. The dramatic difference was that this was a meeting marking a blending together, not a tearing apart. If, in fact, we are certain to always experience both sides of love, which I believe to be true, then this was the other side for Eve and me. We talked from 12 noon until 6 P.M., discussing *A Course in Miracles* and the children's lives during the time that I did not have access to them. Afterwards, Eve invited me to her home to see the girls.

Seeing my girls again after such a long time felt surreal. Hugs and warmth streamed from my heart; my daughters seemed reserved, and unconvinced this would last. From my standpoint, we were on the road to new beginnings.

Priceless Gifts

Christmas of 1999 was fast approaching, and all of us wanted to share in some joint celebration. At our family Christmas dinner, which took place on December 27, all three of my husbands—Adam, Jake, and Allan; all six children; and Eve and I sat together at the dinner table. We did an enormous gift exchange and sat up discussing spirituality until midnight.

During the following weeks and months, I had many discussions with Adam and Eve on the Course and its application. As time passed, however, issues pertaining to some of Eve's previous behaviors began to surface. Eve frequently resisted allowing me time alone with the girls, and whenever possible, she would include herself in our plans to be together. Once again, I felt her need for my approval and inclusion as "a friend." Just as before, I felt her abandonment issues taking over the family dynamics.

Eve suffered from deep feelings of guilt and self-hatred for her actions in the previous 14 years. I would learn this later because she and Adam disclosed that at the time she received my letter, she was deeply depressed and becoming more and more unresponsive to daily living obligations. Adam also said that Eve had not originally planned to respond to my letter—in fact, she had thrown it out. It was Adam who later discovered it, and he just *knew* he needed her to respond. After some urging, she agreed, and responded.

About a year after we reconciled, Eve told me that she had felt haunted for years by various incidents, such as repeated hang-up phone calls, someone filing reports about her and Adam being involved in income tax evasion, and other suspicious occurrences. Eve had believed that all those things were coming from me.

Consider that what we project we perceive, and projection stems from deeply seated feelings of guilt. Eve had projected all the shadow parts of herself onto me. I later gave her proof of my exact whereabouts at the times of particular incidents that she had documented and that she believed me to be responsible for. She was so obsessed in her belief that I was trying to drive her crazy that she had installed a security system and a special phone line with caller ID, so that she would be able to catch me.

Her feelings of guilt were slowly draining so much life force from her that she was becoming ill. She confided that, at the time she received my letter, she had been hoping to die soon, and was consciously trying to create either cancer or a brain haemorrhage, of which her mother had died.

Let's sidetrack for a moment, and look symbolically at the biblical story of Eve, the Serpent, and the Garden of Eden. The Garden represents an equilibrated mind at peace. Eve and the Serpent are in conversation. The Serpent represents the ego-orientated thought system. The lie the Serpent told Eve referred to God's wanting to limit Eve's knowledge—and thus her power.

Consider that the more we love and appreciate who we are, the more authentic power we hold. The more we are willing to see the two sides of people and circumstances we encounter, the more knowledge and wisdom we gain. The more we do both, the more we understand the Great Orchestrating Design, or Love, which is unceasingly offering us the opportunity to appreciate its all-encompassing presence.

It is not God who withholds knowledge; it is limited perceptual thinking that does. So, let's review how the lower, ego-orientated thought system operates. Another symbolic meaning of the lies of the Serpent that the original Eve encountered in the Garden of Eden refers to Eve's needing to embrace her full self, and appreciating the two sides, the side of herself she liked and the side she didn't—the light and the darkness of her full nature.

Remember both sides are perceptual, because both are determined by the *values and goals* of the particular field of consciousness or the being that does the observing. *The evaluation is done based upon perceived, not actual, lack.*

The problem we all face is twofold. First, we unconsciously believe that our individuality comes with a price tag—the price is the guilt we feel for the desire to be an individual; and second, we want to be "special"—different and better than others. This is to deny the true nature of our being, which is holistic, meaning all-encompassing. Because we do experience ourselves as separate, we have a deep-seated belief that our singular identity defines a betrayal of what God created us to be.

Our pursuit of the deepest meaning of love has as its components the full integration and appreciation of the over 4,000 character traits that each of us possesses, as Dr John F. Demartini points out in his book *The Breakthrough Experience*™. He outlines in brilliant detail how every trait is paired to its opposite. Based on quantum theory as it applies to light, he concludes (as other brilliant thinkers have done) that both sides are necessary aspects of having an incarnate physical experience.*

For both the Eve of the Bible and the Eve of this story, susceptibility to fear arose primarily from "secrecy"—a wish to keep hidden some of their thoughts and desires. Once we realize that everything in the cosmos is a part of and thus serves love, there is no longer anything to hide.

MOTHER'S DAY 2000

In the year following my reunion with the girls, I continued to try and teach Eve that, no matter what she thought she had done, she was still worthy of my love and that of the children.

The morning of Mother's Day, I awoke with a song in my heart. Soon after, Joe and Jeremy walked in to serve me

---

* Because we are in "form," we are also governed by its laws—Nature's laws. Therefore the cyclical nature of birth, preservation, and death is inherent within our being. Since the entire physical universe is really an emanation of "frozen light" experienced as solidness, "light" law governs it. The laws that govern light have much to teach about the mind. For an in-depth, easy-to-understand explanation of quantum physics and human consciousness, please read *The Dancing Wulie Master* by Gary Zukav and *The Breakthrough Experience*™ by Dr John F. Demartini.

breakfast in bed. I thought about how sweet they were and how they had, in so many ways, kept me sane and focused on the present. I was grateful for so much.

Later that day, I watched the clock. Hour by hour, I was hoping for a Mother's Day call from my girls—they had not called me on Mother's Day for many years. Hours passed, but no call came, and my heart began to sink. After dinner, the phone rang—it was Eve. "Happy Mother's Day," she said. "We are just down the street and wondered if we could stop by." Ten minutes later, they arrived—Adam, Eve, and the children. Eve said that she had wanted to surprise me. She wanted us to celebrate my first Mother's Day with the girls together. I was heartbroken, but remained polite. I knew things would not last, after that.

THE LAST CALM

Months passed quickly. Tasha and I were spending more and more time together. I helped her to get a cell phone; she called me almost every day. Then the calls stopped. Tasha became more and more unavailable; then her old shadow side began to reemerge. She switched gears and began acting as though I ought to be grateful that she was around. One day, we had a confrontation while driving out to our house. A repressed rage began to emerge from within me, and I lost my calm. I told her she had no idea what it felt like to walk in my shoes and that, if we were ever to have a loving relationship, she would need to put as much into it as I did. I flipped the car around and dropped her off at Adam and Eve's house. I cried all the way home.

I knew in my heart that the inherent danger of this

dynamic was my becoming too soft, too compliant, and thus used. I had feelings and needs also; I needed to risk losing the girls to own my integrity.

I called Tasha a few days later. She said she was sorry and that I was right—she did need to put energy into our healing as mother and daughter. We began again.

From all my children, Tasha is the most like me. Astrologically, we are both Libras, both somewhat moody, and both always willing to start over. I taught her the Course principles; I shared what had really happened all those years she was gone, and we became close.

PURGING THE SOUL

In a moment of sanity or desperation—I am not sure what inspired her—Eve finally confessed the story of our past. She said she trusted that no matter what she had said or done, we would all love her. She wanted to confess all the cruel things she had done all of those years. She sat with each of the girls and shared what she had really done and felt. She cleansed her soul, her heart and mind, and they just listened. She told them that she had been terrified of their loving me more than her—terrified that one day they would leave, and that she was "not good enough" as a mom.

The girls were not surprised by Eve's confession because somewhere in their hearts, they had known this all along. She finally admitted that I had never abandoned them. She had lied about the aggravated assault and other incidents. Meanwhile, Adam denied everything she confessed to. She was now trapped between two worlds, and only one way out would save her.

By late October, Tasha was starting to see the manipulative and controlling nature of Adam and Eve. She could not believe that she had been so blind. I reminded her that they were still being driven by fear.

A week later, Adam called to tell me that his van engine was gone. The van had been Adam and Eve's only remaining form of transportation, and he could not afford to get it repaired. I offered to pay for the repair, and he could pay me back later. He accepted, and we carried on. A month later, I suggested that the easiest way for Adam and Eve to repay the $5,000 loan was for me to suspend child support payments until it was paid off. They reluctantly agreed. They had hoped that, since Allan and I were financially comfortable, we would just "gift" the loan. Allan and I had discussed this option, but decided that we did not owe them anything, and we were already contributing to the girls' physical needs in the way of cash and clothing.

Interestingly, since I had returned into Adam and Eve's life, they had had a long string of mishaps, including a car accident; transmission problems in Adam's jeep, which they could also not afford to get repaired; health issues; and finally the van engine, which was the most costly. It was as if the cosmos was saying, "It's time to tell the truth about the past."

One October evening, I received a call from Tasha. She was sobbing hysterically. Her relationship with Adam and Eve had become seriously strained because she refused to allow them to continue intimidating her. There was verbal abuse, and eventually a physical fight. I knew from what I had witnessed on the driveway three years earlier what their fights looked and sounded like. Tasha told me that at one point in this fight, Adam had her pinned against the wall, holding her by the throat. She kicked him off and ran to her room. Finally, she found the strength to stand up to him, and in her heart, she decided then that she would move out.

During the next month, she became reclusive. Adam and Eve suspected that she was planning a move. This infuriated them, and tensions mounted.

By December, Tasha could no longer bear living there. She often remarked about Eve's sarcastic comments about me. Eve was becoming increasingly jealous. She told both Emma and Tasha that I had staged the whole year of appearing so caring, just to get them back. Both girls began to see more and more clearly the distortions of Eve's thinking. Sara remained oblivious to it all.

Emma and Tasha always said that there had been enormous favoritism in their house because Adam and Eve's son and Sara were allowed to live by a whole different set of rules.

Emma, who would be graduating from high school the following May, had also recently announced her intention to move out right after her graduation. Both Tasha and Emma were no longer willing to endure the disabling control and emotional manipulation to which they had been subjected. Adam and Eve's control over the girls' decision-making processes was fading; they were reverting to their old ways of intimidation and fear to get the children to comply.

TASHA COMES HOME

Tasha called me at the office one day—she was hysterical, crying, and asking me to pick her up right away. I called

Allan, who was on his way home, and asked him to pick her up. Allan arrived at Adam and Eve's house to find Tasha terrified that Adam or Eve would come home before she could get away.

Later, Tasha explained the unfoldment of the events leading to this outcome. She said she had asked for a family meeting to discuss her wish to move out. Then, that day after school, she had found Eve sobbing at the kitchen table and asked her why she was crying. Eve answered that she had done her best, but that now it was "time to go." Eve said, "You now have Moreah and no longer need me. I left a note for your father." Tasha became frightened and asked what Eve was talking about. She had long realized that this was the way that Eve controlled the family. She often threatened to leave when she was not feeling appreciated or validated. She then questioned Tasha about whether she was planning to move in with me, and Tasha admitted that she did want to try this to see how it would feel. Eve became hysterical and left. Tasha ran upstairs, called me, and stuffed everything she wanted to take into garbage bags. She was terrified that Adam would come home before she was gone.

An hour a later, Adam called. He was furious and unreasonable with me. He again said that he would find a way to get back at me, and end my relationship with the girls. I hung up the phone, knowing in my heart that my dance with him was over!

The girls, Emma and Tasha, would attempt one more time to patch things up, but that attempt, too, would fail because of Adam and Eve's continued dishonesty about past events and their desire to remove me from the children's lives. A year later, Emma moved in with us, too. In the fall of 2002, Adam left Eve, taking Sara with him. A year later, he told Eve that he wanted a divorce. Currently, Sara and I are slowly creating a bridge to meet on. Sara speaks with and sees Emma and Emma's son, but has not yet reconciled the truth with Tasha. Tasha remains clear that until Sara wants the real truth about what happened, she is unavailable for a sister relationship. Eve continues to pursue a relationship with Emma and her son. Emma monitors the flow of both.

Reflections on the Dance

The dance with Adam and Eve was both the most difficult and the most awe-inspiring. I learned so much about my nature, so much about the archetype of Mother, and so much about love.

The wisdom I offer from this experience is to remember that love does not possess. It gives freely; it embraces and encompasses all things, including the darkest thoughts we hold. If I am asked if I could do it over, would I? I don't know, but I do know that I would not give up the love and wisdom I gained from doing the dance.

I am not sure what I would have done had I been in Eve's moccasins. Perhaps I would have taken the same steps if I had also had the same experiences as Eve in the years prior to our dance. Remember that in your brother, you will find yourself or lose yourself, depending upon whom you seek. Eve, more than any other individual, helped me find love and appreciate all of me. . .and all of the Great Orchestrating Design!

If the doors of perception were cleansed,
everything would appear to man as it is, infinite.

William Blake

Part Two

Introduction

Although there were opportunities because of what many may call challenges through my dances with Adam, Eve, and the children, so, too, were there incredible blessings and gifts that I am certain were the other side of those "challenges." It is the awareness that each side made the other possible that allowed me to move forward from a place of inspired certainty in "the Plan."

As most people do, I went through my moments of despair, but, as I have shared, those moments simultaneously propagated a deeper searching, a deeper quality of questioning, and deeper wisdom and understanding of how the Great Orchestrating Design functions.

I now offer the other side of my Dance!

CHAPTER 17

Creating a Mystic

My most accelerated period of awakening occurred just prior to, and during, Allan's and my two-month separation in 1994. In that time, I was truly transforming from an immature fluctuating fifth- and sixth-sensory student into a mature, stable, and integrated sixth-sensory student and teacher.

One of my most profound dreams occurred around that time: I was lying on the operating table; there were mystical, magical beings of light all around me. I felt no fear, just intrigue at what they were preparing to do. Then a being of light, radiating intense love, placed his hand through my flesh and pulled out my heart. The light beings seemed to be working on it—a mystical surgery of sorts—I felt no pain, but *remembered* that this was necessary for the work that lay ahead for me.

Then, with the same ease that my heart was lifted from my body, it was returned through my flesh, pain-free. Then a surge of profound joy and an unexplainable readiness fell upon me; I felt as though I had been initiated, but into or for what, I was unclear about.

To the degree that this dream seemed to embrace and support my mystical awakening and psychic abilities, the Old Hag* challenged it. The Old Hag lingered near me at night; she often made her way into my dreams, but was also present when I was awake. She ignited within me horrific fear. She represented all the ancient hate and powerlessness I had ever felt. Her presence forced me to look and find that on some level, I felt that I was abandoned and left in the shadows. She never spoke; she just showed up to test my faith in love, my faith in the mysterious black void–which is also part of God, and my knowingness that both darkness and light are always necessary to evolve the soul. Through the Old Hag, I learned that even the light that seems eclipsed in the darkness is transitory and of God.

During this mystical awakening period, I was reading two books in depth: *A Course in Miracles* and Barbara Marx Hubbard's *The Revelation: Our Crisis Is a Birth*. I was reading anywhere from six to ten hours a day. I had an insatiable hunger to understand the metamorphosis I was under-

---

* The Old Hag is an entity gathered of our disowned parts–she represents our fear of aging, dying, mysticism, mystical power, and the unknown, and she fuels our desire to rise above the astral realm into the realm of Christ Consciousness. The Old Hag often acts as a passageway to separate the student and the teacher.

going; I wanted to stop feeling crazy. I was seeing auras around people, seeing etheric beings, reading people's thoughts—without trying and, strangely enough, seeing the "face of Jesus Christ in people's faces." I searched and searched, trying to figure out what was going on. Although I was not afraid, I was certainly curious. I wanted scientific answers and believed they were there to be found, because I had long since recognized that the Great Orchestrating Design was the Scientist of scientists!

Ever since I was a child, I had been able to converse with angels and guides, so this was not really anything new. What was new was that I had to understand and integrate the process of opening the "third eye" at will. I needed to manage my telepathic, intuitive, and psychic abilities. And I needed to burn through the "ring of fear" associated with misunderstood mysticism and the occult.

The "ring of fear," as I call it, is learning how to confront our darkest thoughts—our own darkest demons, and loving them. What we call dark thoughts or demons are really only differing degrees of "shaded" and unloved aspects of our own nature projected outward. The driving force that these dark thoughts stem from is the unequilibrated, guilt-dominated part of the mind.

Consequently, then, the integration process can indeed feel paralyzing if we do not have enough certainty about what makes up the totality of love (meaning the perfect synthesis of two equal and opposing sides) and feel confident in its all-encompassing presence.

THE THIRD EYE AND MYSTICAL PHENOMENA

As part of our spiritual awakening process, we often experience a deeper awareness of our ability to see energy information. It allows us to see auric fields, and to experience that we are truly magical beings of light. This process is referred to as the "opening of the third eye." When this occurs, we come to realize that, up to this point, we have only been experiencing a small percentage of our total reality. In this sense, we transform from our humanness into our spiritual awareness.

The opening of the third eye will include things like "light episodes" seen as flashes of light, peripherally; seeing a thin track of light around physical objects; and seeing physical objects appear more transparent or living than static and lifeless. The opening of this "psychic eye" is often accompanied by fear, because it involves the unknown and the ego, which, unlike the spirit, hates the unknown.

Let me recount that the ego is a persona that thinks it is you. It is a fractured idea of the true self that operates from the lower split-off mind, rather than the higher, all-inclusive mind. It is founded on the belief that it is self-created, rather than extended from the Great Orchestrating Design. It embodies separation and defensiveness, and encourages us to believe that we are limited and a body, rather than boundless spirit. It is capable only of entertaining half-truths, because it only wants one side of the coin we have called love; therefore, it perceives, rather than knows, anything.

Accordingly, the process of awakening or becoming enlightened involves integrating and appreciating both sides of everything we encounter. It means that we have finally begun to trust the implicate order of the universe. Consequently, it means we begin living many more moments in the now, rather than fluctuating between past and future, fear and guilt. We are no longer trying to avoid anything or anyone, therefore, we are using our life force to attract and appreciate, rather than manipulate, what we do not love.

In my repeated accelerated periods of awakening, I felt an indescribable connection and oneness to all living things. The colors were brighter, crisper, and clearer, and I often felt as if I were in a vivid dream, because there was an accompanying sense of insignificance to whatever I was doing as it related to the Big Picture. In other words, daily tasks seemed minimal compared to a larger contract that I had signed up for. I often spent hours a day meditating and doing yoga, to stay grounded. During the awakened periods, I knew that, no matter what happened, it was part of the Divine Plan.

Then, slowly, the fog and sleepiness would return, and again I would be on the endless cycle of transformation, between knowing and seeing order, and then back into what I perceived was chaos and ignorance.

For the most part, I was experiencing an ongoing unveiling of my true identity. With each cycle, I became a little more confident in the power of the process. Often, it felt like I was being carried by an innate wisdom that fluctuated between times of dormancy and activity within me.

Therefore, during the period that Allan and I were separated, I trusted implicitly that we both were doing what was *necessary* for our mutual growth and for the life ahead—even though I didn't see the details of that life.

Allan didn't understand why I was so calm and certain that everything was going to be fine for us. He often mistook my certainty for arrogance (a mistake that many make!), and he also felt that Lance was in the wings, keeping me busy. Because Lance and I had such strong feelings for each other when we were together, the question of whether we might be soulmates arose in my mind.

So, I'd have to admit and confirm that Allan's suspicions were in part right because I had wondered if Lance was my soulmate. I have long since given up asking the question altogether, trusting that everyone is my collective soulmate, since everyone is helping me to love and integrate my perceived fragments and unloved self. I do acknowledge that there is one single individual who is the mirror image of our soul, but need to also acknowledge that the probability of finding this individual in one's lifetime is minimal. Before we are actually prepared to meet our individual soulmate, we must first have undergone a series of dances with many individuals, both male and female, that have served us to integrate and love all the parts of our being. The more we have integrated our traits of being through our collective soulmate, the more we are prepared to dance with our individual soulmate. I will discuss what I have learned about soulmates in chapter 21, *The Truth about Soulmates*.

While Allan suffered immensely at the thought of losing me, our life, hopes, and dreams, I did not. Not because I had Lance in the wings, but because I was certain that we were like Michelangelo's statue of David inside the marble, and this experience was chipping away the unnecessary marble to reveal our inner brilliance, and our destiny.

I knew that we had begun, as all relationships do, as a *Special Relationship*.* But I also knew that our long-term success as a couple was dependent upon our engaging and participating in a *Holy Relationship*. If Allan was willing to involve spirit in our relationship, I was willing to dance. If he was not willing–and he had originally said that he wasn't–I was off to find a partner that would.

I had been in lots of relationships that had minimized the power and place God had within their fabric, and I was now no longer willing to settle for looks, power, or money!

The fundamental difference in the two forms of relationships is that the *Special Relationship* is founded on "unatoneable" guilt and a deep-seated belief that we are inherently worthless–a belief that we use extreme effort to avoid encountering. The *Special Relationship* is really a counterfeit love. As a result, the relationship has as a basic requirement the need to protect each other from the constant yet unconscious feelings of guilt. All is well in this relationship until either becomes exhausted with the task, or either begins to see the other as guilty and not themselves. Initially both individuals project their guilt onto anyone but each other, but eventually the projected guilt gets so intense that it begins to also shift to the other person. This is both a predictable and inevitable outcome.

In the *Holy Relationship*, the foundation is diametrically opposed to that of the *Special Relationship*. It is founded on the inherent innocence of both people as children of God.

* For an in-depth understanding of the three levels of relationship–the Special Hate, Special Love, and Holy Relationship–please read my book *Rediscovering Your Authentic Self: Applying A Course in Miracles to Everyday Life*.

It is understood between partners that each has been brought into the relationship to deepen their understanding of love, and their capacity to appreciate all characteristics and traits that each individual has. Each has come to learn that through their union, both will learn how to love both sides of each other, and thus themselves. Consequently, each recognizes that each is, in fact, a mirror reflection of the other's owned and disowned parts. Thus, blame becomes pointless, and eventually love and gratitude take its place.

ILLUSIONS

One of my most profound experiences of awakening occurred one day as I was looking at a painting in our kitchen when, quite suddenly, it vanished into a black hole. The whole image, which was of a group of horses, collapsed inside the frame, and all I saw was "pure potential." It was as if the images, which were refracting light, needed something to absorb it. Moments later, the image returned, and I realized that I had just been given a cosmic lesson. What I was becoming aware of was that I was engaged in a three-dimensional experience with my thoughts. I was being shown firsthand that thoughts are things. We project our thoughts and memories outward, and then perceive and interact with them as if they were outside of us. The truth is, if they were outside of the mind, we would not be able to control them. Therefore, we are in a self-referring relationship with our thoughts and our decisions. Mind stuff is everywhere, and thus, the whole physical universe is really a projection of the perceived separated mind seeking to heal itself. We are all doing this healing individually as well as collectively.

Another way that I received that same lesson three years later was after coming out of a meditation in my yoga room. I often sat in front of the mirrored closet, where I could practice "mirroring," something I learned quite by accident while putting on my mascara one day. I was looking at my lashes as I applied the mascara, when suddenly I felt as if there were someone else, or rather "something more" looking back at me—through my eyes. I jumped back, startled. I tried to gaze again, and again it happened. Then I stared back and asked, "What is happening?" My inner voice replied, "You are viewing the world through the higher rather than the lower mind. This is your Psychic Eye." I gazed some more, and then I began to see distortions in my physical features, then other faces emerged. I felt like these faces belonged to ascended beings that watched over me. I asked, and my thoughts were confirmed.

That day, I had been meditating for about 90 minutes, which was the normal amount of time I meditated every weekday. During the meditation, I felt guided to open my eyes and look in the mirror. I did. I was "gazing" mindlessly, when suddenly a whole series of faces began to appear through the reflected image. This lasted for about three minutes, each face moulding itself into the next. I saw all races, colors, classes, ages, and sexes—ascended masters and mortals alike. Then, lastly, I saw the familiar face of Jesus. No words were spoken, but there was an instantaneous exchange of thoughts.

Jesus said, "All of those images are me, all my faces, all myself. All of this is the Christ Being." My face returned as the only image; I was vibrating frantically, my heart raced with joy; I felt like all that I had studied and intellectualized was suddenly *known*. It was no longer concepts; it was now a cellular integration of true *being*. I knew that every cell of my body was vibrating; I knew that I was in that moment fully awake, fully embraced by loving Intelligence.

I went upstairs and called my closest friend, who was also my yoga teacher. As soon as she answered the phone, I began rambling on about what I had just experienced. She could hear and feel the animation in my voice. I tried to use words to explain what had occurred, but they felt limiting and insufficient as symbols to articulate the profound experience. I said, "Rosemary, there is only one of us here. All is One, All is God, and All is Love!" All of these things we had talked about and believed. Yet, it was not the same; after that morning, those truths became *knowing*–the place from which all subsequent growth would begin.

I was pacing the floor as I spoke, explaining in detail what had occurred. I was sweating immensely, and I felt like 120 volts of electricity were pulsing through my veins, but without any pain. There was such joy and peace, and then stillness; I kept feeling like an ancient memory had returned. I repeated to myself, "I remember, I remember now." Appreciatively, Rosemary listened, and shared in one of my most profound moments ever.

CHAPTER 18

A Modern-Day Mystic

Who would have guessed that my career would begin as a result of a money tree pyramid? Well, it did, although I had no idea then that the cosmic plan included pyramid sales—life is all about sales in that we are always "selling" our beliefs and ideals to others in order to feel fulfilled.

It was the fall of 2001 when my neighbor, Susan, called. She was all excited about having me share in an opportunity to "get rich quick and easy." Now we all know that this doesn't work...or does it? Well, when an idea like this one is offered up to the Great Orchestrating Design to be used for Its purpose, all things are possible.

Susan began by saying, "All you need to do is give $100 to the gal at the top of the list. Then you will need to sign up three others to do the same. In a week or two, you will be at the top of the list and get $800–simple as that." "Sounds suspicious; sounds like a money scheme that always leaves someone in the lurch." I replied. "I will think on it, and let you know." I called Allan, and he said that he was already involved in a money tree at work; he said, "For 100 bucks–why not? Just make sure you can sign three others up." I had no concern about that. I called the gal at the top of my list and made arrangements to get the $100 to her.

She told me that this was only tier one, and that we were to reinvest $500 into the next level and $5000 into the last, "for a total earning of 40 grand." I was stunned. I said goodbye and called Sue back. She said she had no idea of the two subsequent levels, and that she simply would not reinvest. She suggested that I do the same.

I thought about this, but it just did not feel fair. I went to sit down in the front room and pulled out my angel guidance flower cards. I shuffled and shuffled, while asking the question if I should participate. Then, as usual, a number came to mind, and then another. This was a little uncommon. I counted down to each of the numbers, then pulled both cards out, face down. I turned the cards over and received the two highest message cards–*Divine Guidance* and *Abundance*.

I had received messages from both cards before, with overwhelming accuracy in connection with events in my life, but to receive both at the same time meant that something magical was unfolding. I thanked the heavens, committed to do unto others as I would have them do unto me, and I called three friends. All three signed up, and I promised I would help them find other participants.

Next, I turned inward to get guidance and confirmation on whether we should participate or not. My inner guidance said, "Go ahead. Just be conscious of doing unto others only as you would have them do unto you." I promised I would.

Week by week, I became more involved in selling spots in the money tree. One of our obligations was to facilitate and attend "encouragement meetings" in order to attract new members to our "pod," as it was referred to. I was the leader of one such group, and it was the most active and successful of all the groups. I had studied the laws of prosperity and knew that this was a wonderful way to teach a prosperity course.

I lectured weekly, and soon I had groups averaging in size from 30 to 120 people. I taught them that to receive, one must give. I taught them to claim the income and pay tax; to do dream collages of the future they imagined; and to believe in themselves and their ability to create wealth.

I remained involved in the organization for six months and had by then made a name for myself as a good inspirational speaker. Because the truth was that my higher value was to teach the laws of prosperity, and I was wealthy in my own right, I felt no need to continue being part of a money tree organization, and I left this association behind me. Instead, I focused on my new speaking career. Then, out of the blue, on one of the mornings just before I left the group, I was meditating, and suddenly I became aware of the presence of a small voice offering an idea, over and over, "Why don't you make up some business cards and begin doing readings?" I thought it was a joke because I had only ever done one paid reading in my life! The thought repeated and repeated; so I listened.

Well, if there is one thing I have learned, it is to take guidance when it comes! I asked one of the gals from the money tree group if she could make me up a business card with *Angels Answers* as the business name. She agreed.

At the next meeting, I offered out the cards to see if anyone wanted one, not really expecting anyone to take them seriously. To my surprise, almost everyone took one, and a few days later, I received a call to do a reading.

For years, I had seen images around people and had received guidance for them when they asked, but I had never dreamt that I would make a career out of this. I was able to see those who had passed over, and I was, by then, an experienced counsellor of the Course principles—I just had not put it all together, but heaven had!

The calls for readings increased steadily, and within a year, I had to move my office out of the house because of the amount of traffic and phone calls I was receiving.

Doing Readings

My first call for a reading came from Michelle, a friend of my friend Jo's. Jo had been getting mini-readings from me for a while, and she suggested Michelle give me a try.

Jo listened and watched me as she saw my eyes begin to gaze at things not normally visible. For me, doing a reading is like going to see a movie; only I have no idea what the show is about—even after I see it. The pictures I see and describe prompt me to say and interpret what is the guidance for the individual. The person receiving the reading connects pictures to questions and feels that their life direction is being made clearer.

The first image I saw was an old Ford truck, representing confirmation from Michelle's dad that he was, in fact, present. A Ford truck was one of many old vehicles her dad had collected; showing it to me was his way of confirming for her that I was real. "Ford" was also the name of a family member. I saw images describing the nature of Michelle's three children, including the one that was in heaven. I described her husband and the nature of his work. I saw a collage of pictures, and saw and heard some of her loved ones who had passed over, as well as her guides. I told her everything I saw, which all seemed a little strange to me, but made absolute sense to her.

Three months after I read for Michelle, I read for her husband and detailed the impending dismantling and restructuring of his new business that would take a full year to complete. A year later, all that had been predicted transpired. He was initially skeptical, but after his reading, he at least believed that there was more to life than what was visible to physical eyes, and he understood intellectually.

Reading wasn't hard; it just took faith that the messages would come. I realized that my sole responsibility was to just be the messenger, and not judge anything I saw. At first, I wandered between a deep gratitude for being the vehicle through which heaven could communicate to absolute annoyance that I had to do it. This fluctuation was present for the first three years, but has subsided greatly now, although I do admit that it does pop up now and then. The annoyance comes from my ego, which at times believes that I have more important things to do than being a voice for Spirit!

One of my most unusual reading experiences occurred while doing my first reading for a now deeply supportive and caring client. Gene came to see me after her daughter-in-law picked up one of my cards at the women's money tree group. She sat down, and I saw all kinds of anger and violence around her and then I saw, clear as day, a gun. I asked her about all the disturbances and then enquired about the gun. She laughed, not at all surprised, and said, "Oh yeah, that's all about Max; he's my son-in-law, and he and my daughter live in the basement of our home, and there is a lot of fighting. Things are really bad, and that is why I came. I wanted the angels to tell me what to do." Well, the guidance that came through was that she should get her daughter, grandchild, and Max to move out and live on their own. Even though Gene did not initially take action on this advice, her daughter and her family finally moved into their own home 18 months later. There were a lot more fights between the time of the reading and the move, but there was a whole lot of growing and learning about what love does, too!

A month after Gene's reading, Max came to see me. He had never been told the identity of his father, and I did not know that. I never ask for any information; I just ask the person to write down questions, fold the paper, put it away, and then let me answer the questions. I learned this approach from the psychic whom I had consulted while in Florida.

I saw a large native North American Indian standing behind him, who told me that he was Max's father. I said to Max: "Your dad is here." He looked at me, stunned; it had not occurred to him that he could get answers on his heritage. He had come hoping to get answers on the living arrangements with his in-laws and the outcome of his marriage. He had not expected to receive information about his father, whose identity his mother had strictly refused to reveal. I described Max's father and told Max that he belonged to a huge tribe and had a lots of siblings and cousins. I told him his father had been the chief, but had died several years earlier. Max, who had come to figure out how to deal with his in-laws, went home knowing his father's identity. He confronted his mother with this information, and she confessed, confirming everything I had offered as guidance. Two weeks later, his mom came for a reading, and she, too, received inspiring answers.

The readings I have done have been as varied as the dance partners I read for. The gift I get each time I read is the absolute confirmation that we each have loving and caring beings that watch over us. They help us uphold our soul contracts and encourage us to live from the highest within us, yet never pass judgment. Each of us has a guardian angel and at times even more than one. These beings attend to our spiritual growth and celebrate each time we choose love when it would be easier to choose the path of fear, anger, and resentment. These miraculous beings believe in our strength and brilliance far more than we believe in ourselves.

THE TRANSFORMATIVE POWER OF CRUCIFIXION

I would like to share with you two significant stories that take us back to the period about six months after Eve and I reconciled. I was doing my morning ritual of prayer and meditation. The previous day had been difficult. Eve and I got into an argument about the reason she and Adam had sued me for child support. Her feelings were that they had done it in order to not have the girls forget about me; my question was why, then, did they not let them see me? The argument was left unresolved, and I was left feeling betrayed yet again.

While meditating, I began to see an all too familiar image that depicted the way I had felt in the relationship —crucified. I was startled at the vividness of the image. I was hanging on a wooden cross; the nails seemed to be slipping, and I watched a hammer slamming everything into place. I pulled back and wanted to turn away, but couldn't. I just had to see how Eve could slam those nails into my hands and feet. To my alarm, it wasn't Eve that was doing the slamming—it was I.

Somehow this image was powerful in its portrayal of how we believe that we are crucified, when in fact we are transformed. The Course teaches that all things that occur are by our invitation. This was a clear depiction of our insane desire to be crucified.

My most recent experience of the same lesson occurred at Christmas 2002. I had been operating the Angels Answers spiritual wellness center on the upper floor of an old house for 18 months when, quite by error, one of the practitioners, Norm, who was working in the Center announced to my landlord that I would be moving out at the end of my lease period.

The fact that I had stayed in that location all this time was a miracle. The landlord was hard to deal with, and I had decided to close out the center four months earlier because I wanted more family time and because of the expected arrival of my first grandchild.

The announcement of my intention to close the center, and to just operate my practice out of an office, began a surging rally by the practitioners to find a way to keep it open. Many people loved the place—the store and library had become a popular hangout for the spiritually minded community. Then, after being given many promises of support in running the business, I agreed to carry on, but we knew relocation would be inevitable within a year because we were beginning to outgrow our current location.

Even though we had talked at length about the need for a larger space, preferably on street level to attract attention to our store, no such location had been found. Then, when I paid the landlord the July rent, three months before my lease term was up, she announced that, after we would leave, she would be occupying the space we had been renting. I asked for an explanation, and she said that a month earlier, Norm had mentioned our relocation plan. Of course, I asked why she did not confirm such important news with me when she heard it, and she replied she just assumed it to be true.

She was not budging on her decision, so I began scrambling to find a new location. Nothing turned up, but eventually an opportunity to purchase an old brick house was presented. A month later, however, this prospect fell through, and I was left facing the possibility that I would need to close down until a new location was found.

One sunny August evening, as Allan and I were heading home from the football field after picking up my son, we discussed the dilemma. My son, who had overheard the discussion, said with a noticeable certainty, "Why don't you *build* a center?" I replied that building would be ideal, but that there was simply not enough time to do so.

As synchronicity would have it, we had taken the long route home and happened upon a large 14,000-square-foot complex under construction. I asked Allan to stop and pull over. From what we could see, the building seemed perfect. There it was—a building right on the far end of Main Street, built and fashioned to look like an old Victorian home. I remembered having seen the initial digging of the foundation a month or two earlier, but I had never imagined that the building would be up and standing that quickly.

I wrote down the builder's name and number from a sign on the fence, when, quite by surprise, a tall man walked out of the house next door. Although we didn't know at first that he was the owner of the building, my mouth just opened, and I said to Allan, "That's him—go ask if we can see the inside." Allan just looked at me, puzzled, then got out of the truck and went over to speak with the man, who introduced himself as Peter. He was an English chap and very charming. Peter told us that only two units were left. We walked through the shell of one of the buildings and then told him that we could have a floor plan to him within a week. We then confirmed our serious interest in the purchase of the two remaining commercial units, and in my heart, I knew the center had a new home!

I told Peter our time lines, and he said that there would be "no problem." Doesn't every builder say that? So, ready or not, we had to move. On November 8th, 2002, we moved in. We had no lights, ceilings, toilets, water, electric power, heat, and only partial flooring. What an ordeal that was! The staff and I were moving and shuffling stuff around contractors, and dusting store stock and furnishings continually.

We were in a real mess! Tensions began to mount. I was busy seeing clients to keep cash flow coming in, and dealing with contractors, so I had no idea what was really going on in the minds of the staff and practitioners, although I felt the tension. Like everyone else, I can sometimes get lost in the drama of what I am currently pursuing and thus neglect to follow intuitive guidance to take note of other issues or problems that surround me. People were getting testy, to say the least. Soon, bickering began about who got which office, and ultimately, there was outright backstabbing aimed towards me, of which I remained unaware until somewhat later.

By late December, we were seeing the light at the end of the tunnel with all construction issues. We were preparing for a staff Christmas party that day, after which we would close for the Christmas holidays. That same day, I would lose all but one staff (my daughter) and all practitioners. This 4300-square-foot building, all mine to fill and operate! Wow—what a blow!

Days later, as I was still trying to sort out what had happened, I was questioned by one of my staff, Louise, about some money that I was supposed to have given to the Global Renaissance Alliance (GRA) back in October. I was confused, and asked what exactly she thought had happened to the money. Louise replied that Kate, who was the store manager and my friend, had said that I never gave the donation money to the GRA, as I said I did. She said that Kate had told everyone that I was a dishonest, money-hungry person, and that she was going to quit, and suggested they do the same. Kate had told all the staff practitioners and some volunteers that I had kept the money to help cover expenses of our move. I told Louise that this was outrageous, and that I could prove that the money went to the GRA back in October. I told her that it was, in fact, Kate who had written the cheque. Louise was surprised and confused.

What I was being accused of was embezzling cash from a peace walk celebration from which we had gathered entry fees; the total cash collected was $465. I was stunned. I showed the proof of the cancelled cheque that Kate had written. Then I showed Louise a letter of gratitude from the GRA to our center. I reminded her that the letter had been posted on the bulletin board for a month, to share the accolades with everyone. All the proof was given to set the facts straight, but it was clear that the gossip had destroyed trust, and all the relationships ended.

From that experience, I did some deep soul-searching and assessing of my own character. I realized that I had expected the same drive and commitment from my staff that I had as the owner–a foolish and unreasonable expectation, based on the belief that spiritually minded people were different and better than everyone else.

I also believe that many, if not all, of the staff had at some point or other put me on a pedestal, as I had done with them. All of us needed to be levelled into balance. Anytime we have aggrandized an individual, we will also eventually minimize them. We have to do this, because we are not able to sustain extreme polarities for long periods, for the law of love is equilibrium. All people are equal; all people have both brilliance and stupidity; and all of us want just to be loved for who we authentically are.

In the months that followed, I began to understand the lesson these dance partners offered, which was, "Own what is yours, and don't make anyone special." I had made huge financial decisions and commitments based on wishes and fantasies, but most of all because of my deep need to make others happy, just as my staff had wanted to make me happy.

I continue to work on healing my deeply seated belief that I am never quite good enough, and recognize that, with this belief as an unconscious driving force in my psyche, I set myself up for problems if the belief is not kept in check. People who help others get what they want are often placed on a pedestal. It is important to realize, however, that if I help others get what they want, I, too, am getting what I want, so there is really no need for anyone to be made special. Consequently, if I am not careful to keep this pattern in check, I will do this same dance again, until I learn it. My success in staying balanced in people's minds, which in turn means that I can stay in their hearts and not on some pedestal, means I need to put these same people off now and then—to show them as my staff did for me, that I am no better or worse than anyone else. Since people are in pursuit of what they value, not in pursuit of pleasing others, we should simply lighten up and recognize that we are all alike!

Each of my staff had a particular set of values and goals. If I was supporting them, I was great, but if they perceived me to be going against them, I was finished. Remember people are committed to *their* dreams, not yours—unless their dreams and yours are identical. My initial feelings of betrayal soon turned into feelings of gratitude, because these dance partners had offered me the chance to own my dance, and the subsequent dances, too!

The motivation behind our *desire* to be crucified from time to time is again fuelled by our incessant need to be "special." This warped desire is also the wish to mitigate God's judgment that we believe is coming down on us. We unconsciously believe that punishment is our due because we think that our individuality has a price—the expulsion by the Great Orchestrating Design from our true inheritance. Each time we experience some form of perceived crucifixion, it is in order to have someone or some situation seen as an external force "do to us" what we secretly wish to do to ourselves. When we finally realize that both we and our brothers and sisters in humanity are innocent, the pattern of crucifixion will have completed its task.

CHAPTER 19

Being the Student

In the weeks and months following the original staff's departure, I searched for ways to generate enough income to keep the doors at the center open. I sought advice from two individuals, both of whom would lead me to a dance floor sparkling with blessings, and opportunities that I perceived as obstacles.

The first was my psychic friend whom I will call Shanti. Shanti is a well-known author and psychic, who suggested it was time for me to take on some students, who in turn could work from the center and generate cash flow. She suggested a group of students, no more than ten, to study with me and be trained in becoming professional intuitives.

I had never formally been placed in the role of mentor, but I respected her wisdom and listened, trusting again that the Great Orchestrating Design would direct me. I set the intention and prayed for guidance. I received the answer that there would be eight students. Then I was guided to share the offer to mentor with me, with some of my clients. I would know whom to offer the opportunity to by listening for and sensing animation with particular individuals.

I did that, and within a month, I had signed up eight people—six women and two men.

It was interesting because it felt like some part of me had mentored before, and that was the part I listened to. I needed a program outline, so I asked what I should do. The answer came immediately: "Write a brief summary of each module they will learn. These modules will be the keys to self-mastery." I listened, and within a couple of hours, I had compiled the *Inspired Mentoring and Leadership Program*™. Here are the outlined modules that I teach in the program:

This is a 36-week course with 12 keys to learn and apply. Each level will be given three weeks to integrate.

Level One

Setting an Intention

In this level, we will explore how to set an intention, what motivates that intention, and then learn how to negotiate all that seems to come into conflict with it. We will learn the transformative principle and commonly asked question in A Course in Miracles, "What is it for?" Learning about the power of the mind and the creative ability of thought will be deeply focused on. The difference between magic and miracles will be profoundly understood. In addition, we will search for all values and concepts that appear to be blocking our intention from manifesting.

Level Two

Integrating Self

In the second level, we will explore archetypal patterns, create our archetypal wheel, and identify key character defence mechanisms. We will learn that each and every person is in an interactive play with only his or her own hidden thoughts and desires. Through this awareness, we will become acutely aware that the problem we perceive is never outside of us. We will learn how to ask the individual or corporate Soul what its mission here on Earth is, and how its past experiences have paved the way.

Level Three

Disillusionment

In this next part, we will continuously equalize our frame of thinking. The Course teaches that only love is real, and that nothing else exists, and that this is the only path to peace and enlightenment. We will, therefore, collapse the illusion of good and bad in as many people, events, and situations as possible. The Course reminds us that regardless of what our perception reports back to us as real, in reality, the pictures we view are reflections of confused and limited thinking.

Level Four

The Witness and the Power of Attention

In the coming weeks, we will finally be able to become the witness or director, rather than the actor of our life. We will begin to look at the small self and the games it plays, hear its voice, yet not be influenced by it. Through the lens of our authentic Self, *we can compassionately and honestly observe, own, and then integrate all the small selves we encounter personally and professionally. We will pay close attention to the shadow or ego personifications of "others" and the world, without policing in any way. Through this exercise, we will know that we are, in fact, the Self beyond this persona, and that we can, for the first time, look with love and non-judgment on the illusory self. We will discover that through placing our full attention on it, we can dissipate its power.*

Level Five

Intuition and Play

In this period, all our attention will be focused on our intuitive capacity. All people are intuitive, but, like any muscle in the body, intuition must be used if it is to be strengthened. There are three ways in which we receive guidance: 1- Mental, 2- Emotional, 3- Kinesthetic. Each of us will primarily receive intuitive guidance differently, in the same way that each of us will perceive the same color in differing shades. These differences will be a part of the needed information for a particular person, which is why two readers will receive the same information differently. We will spend this period learning through play.

Remember the power of intuition is in you—it is an inherent quality of being. *Learning how to trust your intuitive information vs. wishful thinking will be taught and explored. Mastering this skill will take tremendous trust and effort.*

Level Six

Power or Force

Learning the differing aspects between Power and Force will be explored. Power is magnetic and does not afflict upon others, while force does. Power is a magnetic energy and is likened to knowledge and spirit, while force is dominant and can be equated to perception or ego. Power coincides with the cosmic "law of presence" and the "law of least effort" with maximal result, while force reflects laws of time and space with limited result.

Level Seven

Inspiration vs. Desperation

There are only two motives through which we operate in the world; one is inspiration and the second is desperation. Inspiration comes from living in the present, while fully accepting all things as they are. Spirit has no desire to avoid anything or anyone by leaping forward or running away from the past. This is true because it knows that It is all there is, and that the failure to remember this is what propagates desperation—and the idea of the ego.

The ego, on the other hand, operates through desperation because it either does not want to—or cannot—handle whatever or whoever reflects the shadow parts of self. The ego has, through disassociation, avoided encountering this self. Once aware of these facts, we can consciously choose to "accept as is," or love, all of life. From this foundation, the will becomes free, and an unspeakable creative power emerges. When the human will is in perfect alignment with Spirit and the universe, dormant forces emerge and miracles happen!

Level Eight
Void Births Value

In this level of learning, we will explore the dynamics of how a perceived void drives us through desperation until, one day, inspiration emerges. We will explore this dynamic in the day-to-day interactions we encounter. Together we will make discoveries of what infatuates us and what repels us and why. Because both infatuation and repulsion consume our energy and mind, it becomes a vital discovery to know what causes our vacillating responses. We will apply specific techniques to integrate these polarities to live in the here and now. Synchronicity and coincidence will also be explored and understood.

Level Nine
The Power of Choice

Defencelessness will be taught as a reflection of knowledge and used as a skill towards empowerment. "The student suppresses, avoids, or attacks, while the master *dances with* all *the events, people, and circumstances that arise in his/her life." Choice is a power that not many fully understand. Why people fear it, will be revealed. Our power to accept "as is" will become a powerful tool of transformation. We will remind others, so that we are reminded, of defencelessness as an application towards peace. We will deduce that, in reality, the only real choice is love.*

Level Ten

The Spirit, the Mind, the Body

In this part, we will learn the proper hierarchy of the spirit-mind-body connection. We will uncover how these levels of being interact both as a person, and on a "business body." The importance of understanding the values of the mind in relation to the health of the body will be taught. The chakras as information centers will be taught, and listening to the "lingo" associated with the corresponding chakra will become natural.

Level Eleven

Our Mirroring Relationships

In reality, there is only one of us here. . . This idea will become a foundational brick from which all other ideas and cosmic laws stem. We will begin looking at and into others and begin to see only ourselves. We will come to experience that what we think, both consciously and unconsciously, becomes the play we star in. The fear associated with this reality will be examined closely and collapsed. In addition, we will learn how to communicate our needs and values in relation to others' needs and values, remembering again that reflection is at work!

Level Twelve

Altruism and Integrity

To have, one must give all *to* all. *Spirituality is an altruistic path. We recognize on a deep level that, in reality, there is only one divine and perfect presence. In keeping with this fundamental principle, we want to protect the innocence of others, so that we can retain our own. We will explore this "law of application" at length and examine all the related implications to both personal and work-related matters.*

We began the program on April 15, 2003, and the group would graduate on December 15, 2003. Each of my students needed to commit to a minimum of ten hours per month "in class," or shadowing, with me.

I, or rather the Great Orchestrating Design, had chosen my first group of "students," who each had just as much, if not more, to teach me! They were each a perfect reflection of one of my character natures. Some students represented previously disowned traits and characteristics that had dominated the dance floor of my past. What I knew for certain was that this was really all about dancing with all of these "selves," who were now embodied as my "teachers."

Luke represented my searching nature. The part of me that wanted answers and had learned that material wealth could not satisfy the yearning of the soul to evolve. He represented the part that wants assurances when treading in unchartered waters. He embodied my deepest inner knowing that I could achieve anything I truly wanted.

In addition, Luke helped me to value and love the part of me that loves to procrastinate about the things I think I ought to do, but don't really want to do. He also helped me to understand and appreciate the part of me that believes she is always right!

Jack represented the part of me that is physically attractive; we endearingly refer to Jack as our poster boy, since he is extremely handsome. Jack represented my charismatic nature and the playfulness that many don't pick up on. He also represented my naïve nature—the part that somehow just expects everything will "magically" turn out to be okay. Of course, on the flip side of this outlook is the fact that others can view it as being irresponsible.

Kim reflected my queen-like nature, which has often been perceived as "too good for anyone else." This part also reflected my mom, who always believed herself to be a royal. Kim is undoubtedly brilliant, charming, and highly intuitive. She also had some particularly crucial lessons to learn that paralleled many of my lessons with Adam and Eve. She reflected my inner knowing that, no matter what, we could always choose the road of higher consciousness. The question is always, at what point do we individually do that?

Rachael mirrored my spitfire nature. In so many ways, she reflected how I had been 15 years earlier. When challenged, she brought out dormant forces of wisdom unmatched by anyone else I knew. What Rachael brought back to me to love and integrate was the part of me that, when feeling defeated, so easily succumbs to victimhood, but that can equally show the face of an unstoppable empowered victor. Rachael and I went head to head on a few occasions; each time, I gained more respect for her courage—and sometimes for her self-righteous ignorance, too.

Sharon embodied in many ways who I was in my past and wanted to look like in my future. She is a fifty-plus businesswoman and athlete. She is gorgeous and exudes class and wit. Sharon reflected that, no matter how hard things got, we should still be willing to transform our crippling egoist nature. She reflected many of the ways in which I had become numb, and equally as many ways that I had become warmer in my overall persona. Sharon proved that, when a love relationship ended, child issues could be lovingly resolved and assets fairly divided. She reflected to me the absolute "proof" that any two souls who want to "do unto the other as they would have done unto themselves" become the recipients of success, even in the dance of divorce and separation. She, like Kim, reflected royalty—and all that encompasses it.

Leanne was a mirror reflection of deep caring and compassion. She emanated love, kindness, and warmth. She shone out pure faith in God. She had incredible courage to overcome addictions to life-threatening substances, which she herself admitted to using. She represented my warrior archetype. She had been to hell and back, and had managed to do the journey without being a victim. She reflected the magical child I kept inside and who believed that all things were possible with love.

Jesse represented my "sacrificial" patterns and beliefs—the *personas* that were sacrifice- and martyr-orientated; the parts of me willing to leave a marriage or any deep relationship in pursuit of God, if I felt it necessary in order to evolve.

She represented the trapped and unappreciated aspects of motherhood, my once deeply rooted abandonment issues, and, most importantly, she taught me how to reclaim my self-worth. This lesson, which is one of the most powerful of all soul lessons to learn, was her greatest gift to me. In addition, *Jesse* represented my unexpressed inner teenager, the one who appeared so adult, but was also, in so many ways, craving to be reckless and irresponsible. Jesse has a twinkle in her eye that says, "I believe in you!"

Jenna represented the part of me that most questions the mysteries of life—the part that struggles ceaselessly with "I am not good enough...yet," and "I need your approval first." Jenna made remarkable strides in the eight months we danced; she has an insatiable hunger to know God and is truly committed to finding the answers to life's deepest questions. She is a modern-day mystic willing to turn every stone and spend as much of her personal resources as is necessary to find her treasures.

And, lastly, my short-term student who was a huge support to me just after the staff at my center moved on, *Lace*, taught me to believe in my ability to run a business. She reflected my artistic drive, and my strong phoenix alchemist nature. She and I both believed that anything is possible. Romantically, she reflected the wisdom that pursuing the Great Orchestrating Design does not mean leaving loved ones behind—it means patience and trust in the implicate order and timing of all things.

Each of these dance partners gave gifts far beyond measure, and each has left footprints etched upon my heart. To each of you—thank you!

MASTER JOHN

Many of us have heard the phrase, "When the student is ready, the teacher shall appear!" That is how I felt when I first learned about, and then met, Dr John Demartini, hereinafter referred to as "Master John."

It was late January 2003 when I went to see a colleague and acquaintance of mine, Garry Larson, MD. He and I had met a year before and had conversed on some topics pertaining to the growth and growing pains of our respective centers. He owned and operated an alternative health clinic. Garry and I were discussing the treatment of clients and patients. In particular, we focused on how much of the healing of the body and life was related to the mental, psychological, and emotional stability of the client.

We got on to the topic of the illusion that we believe our life to be disordered. I shared with him one of my techniques for helping depressed or stressed individuals see the other side of what they initially perceived as "bad." I said to him, "Most people don't realize that anything they encounter with someone else that seems disconcerting is really a part of themselves they have not yet loved and understood." Garry sat up, intrigued, and asked if I had heard of Dr John Demartini, a former practicing chiropractor, whom he referred to as brilliant. I had not. Garry said that John Demartini had developed a methodology based on the laws that govern light and had applied it to the human psyche—it is called the *Quantum Collapse Process*™ (The Collapse).

He said it would be right up my alley, and I should read Demartini's book. We continued our conversation, and then I shared in detail the story of what had occurred with my staff the previous month. He replied, applying the *Quantum Collapse Process*™ line of questioning on me; he asked, "What was the benefit of the staff leaving?" I had thought about that at length, and shared my insights. Then I asked, "What about the lies that started the whole spiral?" He replied by asking, "Where do you lie?" I thought about that and then realized: I had lied to myself, and to them. I had lied to my husband, kids, and previous employers. I had lied to clients and to phone solicitors. Suddenly, I realized that I had lied as much, if not more, than my staff had. I knew the next question would be: About whom had I told untruths? Again, I saw that. I had talked, or rather gossiped, about anyone that had put me off. I had spoken unkindly, and, without question, had said things that, from my limited awareness, seemed true, but which I later found to be a lie. I had done everything they had, even at the same time that I perceived they were doing something to me. Next, Garry asked the Great Discovery question. Garry asked, "At the very instant that you were feeling put down, who was picking you up? Who believed in your innocence?" "Me," I said, "and Emma, my daughter, and Allan." Then, like a light bulb bursting, I thought of Cindy, one of my center volunteers, and that she had believed me, too. "Good," he said. "Do you realize that you can't have one without the other?" Yes, I knew from my study of light that both positive and negative charges were inseparably connected. Then Garry said something to the effect that, since I had experienced both sides of a two-sided phenomenon called physical reality, I really had just experienced an interlude with love.

I got it. With a hug and a smile for Garry, I headed on my way. I purchased Master John's book *The Breakthrough Experience*™ and also an audiocassette, *No Such Thing as a Dysfunctional Family*, a recording of a live radio interview with Master John. I made my way home listening to the interview. I was awestruck! I pulled over and cried tears of gratitude. After so many years of asking for a teacher "on earth," I knew with every cell of my being that I had found one. In all my years, I had not heard such an inspiring message. It paralleled everything I had learned as a student of the Course, and it solidified my desire to teach both spirituality and science, since I saw them as inseparable bedfellows. I knew in my heart that I would someday meet my teacher, Master John, and that something profound would come of our meeting.

In the weeks to come, I devoured Master John's book and saw the similarities to all that I had already been teaching in *A Course in Miracles* language. The profound difference was that from that point on, I had an additional vocabulary to draw from.

I began having a series of dreams about Master John just prior to taking his classes and training seminars. Then, one morning, I got the direct order from my voice within to pursue Master John's teachings, which were a culmination of the wisdom he had extracted as vigilantly as I had pursued the Course. I knew from that day on, Master John and I had a dance!

The following months, I studied and learned all that I could. I committed to becoming a certified *Quantum Collapse*™ practitioner, and I made a promise to become an instrument for Master John's message to reach the world.

GETTING THE PART

For me, it seemed as if from the instant I said, "I will" to the request of promoting Master John's work, the universe began to play! It was late June 2003, when one of my clients, Laura, who also works as a promoter of authors and speakers, received a call from a Toronto-based television scout named Chance.

Chance told Laura that her TV production company was creating a new reality TV show entitled *Hooked Up*. The show was a blending of the TV shows Fear Factor and The Bachelor, The Bachelorette. The motivation for all prospective cast members that would be reduced to ten gals and guys for the casting of the program was to see if they could find their soulmate. Chance was calling Laura to see if she knew of any astrologers that could be of help to the cast in identifying who, if any, of the other cast members was their soulmate.

After hearing the requirements, Laura felt that I would be a better candidate, since I could effortlessly read the soul. She felt that both my speed and accuracy would make for some fascinating entertainment. She encouraged Chance to consider me for the guest position, and then called me.

I was interested in the opportunity and I encouraged Chance to pursue it. Months passed with no confirmation about who, if anyone, had been chosen for this role. We had, on our own initiative, done a video of Laura interviewing me, and asking key questions that might spark Chance's and the producer's interest further. In addition, we sent a copy of a live television interview I had done, reflecting the ease and comfort I portrayed and felt in front of the camera. Then, by September, I travelled to Houston to train under Master John, and participate in a certified teacher training program in the *Collapse Process.*

While we were there, we were focusing on the need to increase our proficiency in the proper application and communication of doing the *Collapse* well. As a requirement, we needed to collapse as many issues and people as possible. I chose to do a collapse on my potential participation in *Hooked Up*. I began with noting down all the benefits and drawbacks of doing the show—benefits such as experience in front of cameras, increase in exposure, possible gains for the wellness center, possible lead into having my own show, and so on. The drawbacks were: not being good enough, coming off as a flake, too much exposure and can't meet demands, hard on the marriage, being put on a pedestal, envy, and so on. My partner, Darren, asked the key questions as we went through the benefits of the drawbacks, and the drawbacks of the benefits lists. The clinching question that collapsed both the fear and infatuation around having the spot was, "What is the benefit of failure?" I saw that it allowed me to continue being a student, I was allowed to hone and further increase my accuracy, and, most of all, I would be able to be perceived as equal to everyone else. Darren concluded by reminding me that having a pleasure without a pain was impossible, so, no matter what happened during the filming, I would be experiencing and embraced by love! That did it! I was no longer either wanting or rejecting an outcome; I was psychologically free. The next day, I received a call from my staff. They announced that Laura had called at the end of the previous day saying that I got the part!

CHAPTER 20

Dancing with Spiders

SPIDERS AND THEIR WEBS—SPINNING THE ILLUSION OF TIME

While in Houston, and on the second day of teacher training, I decided that I should *collapse* spiders. As a long-time student of the Course, I felt that I had made peace with most of the people and incidents of my past. Since I had already dealt with the new TV show opportunity, I was searching for something to collapse the illusions around.

At the beginning of the program, Master John spoke to us about the varying personalities and professions of our prospective clients. He told us that those working in psychology and psychotherapy often have a very difficult time working through the Quantum Collapse Process™. I was, of course, one of those individuals. Master John further explained that the final step before transformation is referred to as "indifference." He said that these individuals have studied science or mysticism long enough to no longer believe that they can have a pleasure without a pain, a negative without a positive, or an up without a down. These individuals have become masterful at staying in the middle—or at least they think they have. Master John said that these individuals actually want a pleasure without a pain, but no longer are conscious of that desire.

I found this very interesting. I could relate to it, and I knew what John meant—I called those individuals the "unhealed healers." They usually knew the talk, but disengaged from doing the walk.

When doing a collapse, we often move through many shades of light; from darkness all the way to whiteout. The emotional and psychological scale could move from fury all the way up to silent gratitude. The in-between stages are, "Ah, I am beginning to see parts of them in me," and, "I am exactly the same," to "I am grateful I am that way," and "I understand this so well now that I would love my child or loved one to experience this same dance." The final stage before enlightenment is indifference.

With all that said, I decided to collapse spiders. I knew that I was not quite at the indifference stage with them, yet I was no longer afraid of them, either; I just didn't like them. My goal was to deeply emotionally appreciate their presence in my life, since psychologically, I could already see their importance in the ecology of life.

With all collapses, we begin with a breakdown of the

components, which in our minds make up the person, place, or thing we are collapsing. Since no two people would use all the same components, it is critical to allow the person working through the collapse process to do their own list of perceived components.

My components of the negatives, namely what I did not like about spiders, were: black, hairy, prickly legs, fast, jump, and tickle. On the positive: aware, beautiful webs, artists, and, most important of all, spiders' webs reflect timelessness.

I began the process with Anne as my therapist. Although she is a professional therapist, this was her first experience at facilitating the process of collapsing. We began on the *perceived* positive components sheet, with the word "aware," and she asked, "Where are you aware like the spider? Who sees your awareness—family, friends, colleagues?" I listed lots of people until I could say that I had as much awareness as the spider. We went all across the columns on the positive side, seven in all. When we reached the last column, she asked, "What would be the drawback if the opposite of column one were perceived or present?" The opposite of awareness for me was unconsciousness. My immediate response was being upset because, if spiders were unconscious, then there would be spiders everywhere—they would not be conscious enough to hide and run away. This was an important "aha!" moment. I realized that spiders were as afraid of me as I was of them.

Next, we moved to the *perceived* negative components. The theory behind the idea of looking at both perceived sides is to *"deinfatuate" the positives* and *appreciate the negatives*. Remember that it is all a *game of perception*; in reality, positives and negatives are interchangeable, depending upon who is doing the evaluating or measuring.

The first word in the negative column was "black," so again, Anne asked, "Who sees that you are black?" Again, I had to allow my memory to find all the ways I am black, and who has seen this part of me. *Being black* is again a perceptual question. For me, being black didn't identify my skin color; rather it identified certain parts of my nature and certain characteristics I portrayed. My memory took me back to incidents such as the time when I discovered Eve and Adam in my home while Sara was critically ill and the idea of killing them both had entered my mind. This happened again with my desire to kill Adam when I lived in Port Alberni and Adam refused to allow me to talk with the girls. There were lots of such incidents, and I agreed that I was as black as the spider. The second-column question was, what was the benefit of the blackness of the spider to me? Next was the question, what was the benefit of the blackness to others? All of these questions are geared to reversing habitual thinking patterns; to help us see that there is another side to consider.

Remember that the lower, ego-orientated mind is always one-sided. Each time we are able to ignite a two-sided thought pattern, we begin to see truthfully, and thus become grateful and fully present.

We completed that column all the way across, looking for all the benefits to "black." Once I recognized this, we continued with the next word on the perceived positive side. The next component was "hairy." With the collapsing of this word component came a rushing forward of memories of Mom and my perceived childhood pain. Memories are really unequilibrated experiences, according to Master John, who also explained that when we have memories that are not "charged," or seen as positive or negative, but are rather seen as the synthesis of both, then this is called "reveracy."

I was amazed how the questions prompted various memories of my previous husbands, siblings, parents, and my past in general. It was as if there were a silk strand connecting everything and everyone!

I remembered, in particular, a time that I was sleeping with Mom and, upon awakening, I spotted a curl of her hair lying on the pillow that I perceived to be a big, black, hairy spider. I became terrified, and tears came streaming down my cheeks. I began telling Anne about my perceived painful childhood experiences. She began crying also, because she was a rape survivor, but she had not yet collapsed the incidents, and my life in many ways reflected hers.

Master John, who was overseeing everyone's collapse, spotted us both in tears and obviously confused. He came over and asked what was going on. Anne told him I was collapsing spiders, but that all my memories were taking me back to my most fear-filled, disempowered experiences.

Master John, who was totally unaffected by my uncontrollable sobbing, kept drilling out the questions. He asked, "What do you most dislike about spiders?" "Their prickly legs, and they are fast," I replied. He said, "Where are you fast?" I knew the answer immediately. I was fast everywhere. I got things done fast and was a master at multitasking quickly. Then he asked, "What is the drawback of being slow?" I don't know why he asked me this, but I crumbled. I said, "Oh my God, if I had been faster, I would not have lost my children." I was mortified. I was unconsciously being driven by the belief that if I had acted faster, and not had the nervous breakdown, which paralyzed me for a month, I would still have the girls.

Next he asked, "Where do you have prickly legs?" "I don't," I sobbed. "Yes, you do!" he barked out. "I don't! I shave all the time; I won't even get into bed with stubble!" I was getting angry. I started asking why I kept remembering the horrible stuff from my past. He said, "Quit avoiding my questions; you are good at that. I know people like you—you area masters at evading this kind of work." I hated him. He asked again, "Where do you have prickly legs?" I said, "I don't!" I felt disorientated and sick. He asked me again, "Where do you have prickly legs?" I said, "Please understand—I don't have prickly legs." Next he said, "Where do you have smooth legs?" Suddenly, I saw three sets of smooth female legs—mine and that of two of my daughters, Emma and Tasha…there was one set missing. I was searching for Sara's smooth legs, yet I could not find them. In my mind, I raced back in time, and then I froze at the time that Sara was five months old—the age she was when she moved in with Adam and Eve. Master John asked me, "Where are Sara's legs?" "I can't find them; they're missing," I sobbed uncontrollably. I told him that my former husband and his wife had taken the children 18 years earlier and that only two of them had recently returned to my life. I told him that I had not had a mother-daughter relationship with Sara since they had taken her. His eyes filled with compassion for my perception, yet asked with certainty, "Where is the new form of Sara, then?"

He asked me to see who had taken her place. His line of questioning was based on the truth that energy cannot be created or destroyed; it only transforms. As suffering individuals, our pain of believing that something or someone is missing is experienced largely because we are untrained at breaking down the components or parts that make up the person, place, or thing that we perceive to be missing. We are addicted to specific forms, and resist looking for a new form because, as mentioned earlier, we are really quite attracted to playing out the victim.

In Course language, forms that we are fixated on wanting to have or become are called idols. Similarly, Master John wanted me to give up my addicted perception that Sara could only be in my life in one form and through one individual. I understood and accepted his reasoning, and so I looked and looked until I could see her in the new form. He asked me to break down the components that were in my mind as Sara. For me, Sara was a child, dependent, blonde, beautiful, helpless, funny, innocent, trusting, naïve, loving, caring, and so on.

Next, we moved backwards chronologically through the years, and I began to see clearly all the friends, co-workers, children, clients, husbands, employers, and acquaintances that played out Sara's part in my life. The most recent and current individual that filled her role in my life was my grandson. I could see that she was no longer missing, and suddenly the pain that I had buried deep beneath indifference evaporated, and only a deep sense of joy and gratitude remained.

I was deeply grateful to Master John for walking me back through time to see that nothing was missing. However, I still wanted to understand how collapsing the spider had initiated this journey. I was then obsessed with that quest.

My friend Dr Garry Larson was also attending the

teacher training, and we sat up until late discussing the fascinating way in which the mind operates. I asked him if he felt that I had collapsed the spider, or if it was really only a symbolic figure of a "ghost" memory. He felt that, based on my feeling of gratitude that Sara was, in fact, not then, nor ever had been, missing, I had completed the task. We said goodnight, and I went to my room and then to bed. I tossed and turned for hours, as I was not convinced that I had completed my dance with spiders, but I was exhausted and finally drifted off to sleep.

The next morning, I awoke and did my morning ritual of prayer and meditation. I knew that I had more work with spiders ahead. I asked for a miracle. I also acknowledged that it would be most beneficial for me to be left wondering, I would trust that not knowing was part of the Great Orchestrating Design's plan also.

Shortly thereafter, Garry and I had a morning coffee and walked back to the training room. Again I asked him what he thought about the whole spider deal. He said that when he had returned to his room the evening before, he flipped on the TV to see a documentary on black widow spiders! I knew I had not finished collapsing spiders, and prayed that the day would unfold answers to my question.

As in the previous days, Master John spoke of the mysteries of light, biology, physiology, parapsychology, and so many more "ologies" that I can't remember them all. He talked of many miracles and healings that were the result of people's collapsing their illusions of disorder or abandonment. I listened and then began to notice that I saw spiders in many of the teacher trainee faces.

It was like watching a Disney movie where spiders were

made to have human qualities. I was not at all frightened—I was fascinated. Whatever a person's bone structure or physical features were, the appropriate spider face to that individual's structure would be reflected. Garry was a Tarantula, and there was a red head with strong bony features that reminded me of an African red spider. There was another dark-haired, petite woman who was a black widow, and there were several varieties of house spiders. Brown ones and black ones in all sizes. I even saw a teacher who looked like a wolf spider. I started to wonder if I was losing my mind.

Then, while listening to Master John, I began to fade out; the miracle I had asked for was about to unfold. I don't know what happened exactly, or what Master John said that triggered the collapse, but all the veils covering the truth of my past lifted.

The people in the room began to vanish, including those whom I had in days prior recognized to embody the qualities and traits of key dance partners of my past. One by one, I began to hear and see my dad, stepdad, mom, former husbands, Eve, Sara, and Allan. I was suddenly transported into another dimension, or so it seemed. Time stood still—there was nothing to do but listen. I heard and had a dialogue with each of these significant dance partners, who each said in their own words how they loved me and always had. Of particular impact was what I heard Adam say, which was that he loved me deeply. He said that in his heart he knew the girls were his to be responsible for in order to allow me to pursue God. He said that I could have never accomplished all that I had if they had been with me, and he was glad to have been of service. Sara was next. She said, "Mommy, I love you so much, and I want to thank you for letting me be where in my heart I felt I was meant to be."

One by one, I listened to these "soulmates" express their love and reveal the contracts that we held. I have no idea how long the collapse lasted; I only know that when I had finished listening and saw with crystal-clear understanding the divine order that my life had always been in, I had no choice but to express my gratitude. I stood, and as Master John continued teaching, I walked over and hugged and thanked each individual who represented the current form of a loved one from my past. They included Garry, who was the new form of my second husband, Jake, and Tom, who is both a client and a friend who had also traveled from Calgary to do the teacher training. Tom was the new form of my dad, and I had told him this a couple of times. I thanked each individual. The last person I hugged and thanked was Master John, when he was finished presenting for the morning. I knew from the first moment I watched him present that he was the new form of Adam.

He thanked me for being so transparent, so open-hearted, and for not stopping until the whole collapse was done. He concluded by saying, "You will touch millions of lives."

That afternoon, several people came up to me and described the light and glow around me. They seemed to be trying to articulate something like, "Thanks for demonstrating for us what love can do when it is undistorted by lies."

CHAPTER 21

The Truth about Soulmates

During my accelerated period of awakening that occurred while Allan and I were separated, it seemed that I had an open door to the *Akashic Records*, also known as *The Book of Life*. I asked some of life's deepest questions then, and it was made clear to me that the Great Orchestrating Design does not wish to keep anything from Its creations. And, as Master John states so well, "The quality of the answers we receive is based upon the quality of the questions we ask!"

At one point during this period, I asked how souls were made, and to my wonderment, I was shown the answer. Since words are often inadequate to properly describe the wonders of the Great Orchestrating Design, the process of how souls are created was shown to me in telepathically communicated imagery. I shut my eyes and saw what appeared to be a galaxy, although it was not really that—a galaxy is just the closest thing I have to compare to what I saw. There was a velvety blackness, and out of it came incredible bursts of light, which then split. I understood the light to be a "beingness," and it was somehow androgynous. Then, quite magically, it refracted out of itself a twin light that I perceived to be male or female, depending upon which dominant traits or qualities it sustained in its dominant presence or being. I sensed that these two mirror reflections were in communication, although I heard nothing audible. I sensed that each was also a mirror reflection and expression of something greater. Not in the sense of this being something better, but rather something more ordered, conscious, and intelligent.

The soul looked somewhat like a star—but not quite. There was a feeling of a chorus of attending "light-being figures" witnessing the process. It seemed not really as much of a physical phenomenon as a mystical one.

I sensed that this pair of souls was to embark upon an endless journey, and would one day be one of these attending beings. I felt the attending beings were like parents or midwives—this seems to be the closest possible explanation. I knew somehow that each of these souls was to separate from its partner and dance an endless series of dances until there would be no part of themselves, or what appeared as others, that they did not love, understand, and appreciate. Time to accomplish this task had no meaning, for the certainty of the accomplishment was inherent.

I sensed that these two beings were alike, yet opposite. They were drawn to and expressing in opposition to each other. I knew that both were whole in and of themselves, but since they were of "One Light," they would one day return to each other fully loving, appreciating, and understanding all things of the flesh. When this would be accomplished, they would then reunite and together be able to create "Light" that reflected their soul.

Each would journey to the land of flesh and live under its illusory spells of separation and loss. Each would encounter other souls who were contracted to help each of them fully love and appreciate all aspects of themselves—both the feminine and the masculine. Since there were indeed things that these "young souls" did not yet understand and appreciate about themselves and the Great Orchestrating Design, there was much to learn, and many souls to dance with. Since, however, energy is never really created or destroyed, but rather transformed into higher and higher states of awareness and order, each soul would really always be surrounded by the components of its mate. When the soul recognized its mate in the many and no longer yearned for what it already had, a sound "like the sound of a trumpet" would sound in heaven, and each soul would begin the journey back towards each other.

Because there were such differences in what each would learn to love about itself and in the rate at which this was accomplished, the possibility to encounter, yet not recognize, each "self" was predictable. Therefore, there were three deities ordered to attend to each soul pair. The deities were those of *Necessity, Compassion,* and *Choice.* Their purpose was to assist the pair to encounter and embrace its most fractured and disowned parts, just as they had once helped me to learn how to love and to forgive the belief in my guilt. To the degree that each individual soul could integrate itself, to that same degree did it also facilitate that same integration for its mate, even though this mate was dancing a different dance at that particular time. In other words, any advancement by either soul would have an immediate effect on its mate.

The soul pair would rarely be together in the flesh, although they would be able to help each other from the nonphysical dimension. The final return to each other was sped up only through the increased awareness that there was no part or characteristic unworthy of loving and appreciating within them.

The vision and dialogue ended, and I stopped looking for my mate, by whom I knew myself to always be inseparably surrounded.

THE LAST DANCE

Our final Dance is one in which we learn that "the dance," the dance floor, the music, and the participants are all ultimately we ourselves. They are all projections of our deeply seated guilt, born of the belief that we could dance apart from God. Miraculously, however, through the dances we *remember*, and thus the dream dance slips silently into the nothingness from which it came. You see, in the Last Dance, we return to love, being formless, timeless, and spaceless; we remember who we are, and that our identity is unalterable. We awaken, having learned that the deepest meaning of love is to acknowledge that we are all wholly innocent, brilliant beings freed from the belief that we ever separated from our Source, our Substance, and our Supply.

Part Three

The only thing we have to fear is fear itself.

Franklin D. Roosevelt

Sacred Trust

LEARNING THE LANGUAGE OF THE PSYCHIC MIND

We have all heard the phrase "a picture says a thousand words." In my childhood or early adult life, I could never have imagined the depth that this particular phrase would come to have in my life. In this section of the book, we will be exploring symbolic images and what they mean to the clients for whom I read. I have come to understand, through doing hundreds if not thousands of readings, that the mind, spirit guides, angels, and teachers use pictures as a way of communicating information, and uncovering our states of ambiguity and confusion.

When I read, I always pay close attention to the feelings that are aroused by the pictures seen. If I see the picture, I offer the guidance, because I trust that the individual is ready to hear the information. I also trust that I would not be shown the picture if the individual were not ready to receive what is given.

DEATH

If I see a death while reading for a client, I offer that information as well, and explain that there are both physical and symbolic deaths to consider as possible outcomes. Because a reading is picking up on the energy patterns or thoughts of the client before the incident or illness occurs, I remind the client that a change in their thoughts can create a change in effect, provided there is no higher way to learn or transcend a particular lesson. Further, I make it known that it is not the individual that dies, but rather that their energy is transformed. The spirit is moving on, and it is only the body that is being laid aside, so that its particles can be used by another consciousness seeking form in the future.

CAR ACCIDENTS

When I see a car accident, I note the place the car was impacted, as this is an indication of where the driver is investing too much life energy. See the *Glossary* at the end of this section for specific impact location details. All impacts define the importance of living in the present moment.

SUICIDE

One of the more common concerns I discuss with clients pertains to individuals who have committed suicide. The prominent questions and concerns are: Where do these souls go if they have embarked upon such a journey? And are they punished for not valuing the physical life more than they did? By the very nature of these questions, we can acknowledge that we have been somewhat "dramatized" into the belief that these loved ones are doomed to damnation.

However, damnation of any kind is not what I experienced with my own suicide attempt. Nor has any individual with whose spirit I have psychically communicated experienced damnation for the relinquishment of their physical body. The fundamental lesson they were learning is like our own: *As I think, so shall I experience!* For these individuals, the understanding that it was the power of their thinking that was driving their subsequent experiences is the liberating factor. As they come to appreciate their own inherent and "unadulterable" innocence and beauty, they are able to release their guilt. If, on the other hand, that connection of innocence is not made, they are most likely to fall prey to the demands and guilt that the ego incessantly lays upon them. In such a case, death seems to be the most merciful option for all involved.

Some individuals who survived their own suicide attempts had a very different experience. The images they encountered were reflective of hell and damnation, which in truth were mirroring the unhealed guilt within them. For these individuals, a continuation of the journey into the spirit world ultimately reveals their innocence. Through my own personal experience with suicide, both as a participant and as a psychic who communicates with those passed-over loved ones, has shown me that their core desire was that they wanted to be loved and appreciated for who they were—not who others expected them to be. From the other side, they finally recognized that their loved ones wanted the same thing they did: love and appreciation. Most remorse picked up around this issue, then, is in the sadness of the realization that something so simple and obvious as wanting to be loved is so overlooked.

As I shared earlier, after my own suicide attempt, I was clinically dead for a while. In no way did I feel judged or damned for my decision to end my physical experience. It seemed somehow understood by all my guides, angels, and teachers that my arrival in that realm of consciousness we refer to as heaven occurred as a result of my feeling that there was no other option available to me in order to feel free and appreciated.

In their opinion, I had not done anything "'bad"–I had just lost my power to reason and see the two sides of the situation I was creating. My decision to end my physical life was fuelled by the desire to move out from beneath my perceived entrapment. If I had had the power in that moment to see the many ways in which I actually had freedom, such as a driver's license and a car, for instance, I would probably never have made that decision.

However, since this was not the case, I was fortunate enough to experience first-hand the suicidal mind frame and consequence–perhaps so that I could work with surviving loved ones and the souls that have been touched by this dance. What I know for certain is that all souls are miraculous reflections of the Great Orchestrating Design, and that they are beyond its judgment and condemnation.

I offer my realization that we are addicted to forms and, in particular, we believe in the importance of the bodily form. The body is meant to be a learning instrument for the growth of the eternal soul. The lesson of the soul is always twofold and always the same: to deeply know thyself and to love thyself as God does. Consequently, when we no longer feel able to do this, we choose physical death rather than live in a state of self-disgust and guilt. Even those who are creating and experiencing fatal illnesses are on some level making the choice to die. Blame towards someone for such a choice comes from misunderstanding the proper use of the body as a tool of learning for the mind. Since the body is a tool towards learning, the tool should never precede the importance of the learner, the lower mind. The learner is the part of the mind that has forgotten its identity. The soul has not, and never will.

The Language of the Soul

The glossary on p. 261 lists some of the symbolic images that I see when I do readings for clients, and which I have come to understand to be the language of the soul. My hope in sharing this glossary is that, as you awaken your own symbolic sight, you may come to understand the language of your soul also.

I offer this part of the book through the Holy Spirit,

whose constant and abiding voice helps me to bring clarity and courage to others through the communication of pictures, words, and feelings.

May you discover your innocence and thus your true Self. Amen...And So It Is.

Until you know that life is inspiring,
and find it so, you haven't found the message of your soul.

Anonymous

Glossary

A

Alchemy. Pouring gold: turning tragedy into triumph.

Alice in Wonderland. Archetypal message about integrating the self. Usually the individual wants to run or hide from something or someone in his or her life. They may perceive the grass to be greener on the other side.

Angel. Divinely guided, not alone.

Ant. Disciplined, hard worker; altruistic.

Apples. Seeking knowledge, or time to take a bite out of life!

Ashes. Burning away the old; transformation; seeds of new beginnings.

B

Baby. New life, new beginnings, innocence.

Back. Ability to stand up, uphold one's honor code; if bones look brittle, person is feeling powerless.

Back burner, stove. Person is avoiding something or has not yet fully committed to task at hand.

Backhoe. Unearthing and/or healing the past; excavating what is real or true; ploughing up your foundation.

Backing up (moving backwards). Afraid of intuition, the unknown; sensing a disowned part of self in others.

Bat. Psychic sensing, entering the void, finding and healing shadow self, birthing new beginnings.

Birds. Wings to fly; look at situation from above.

Black. Pure potential, void, mystery, private agenda when associated with a person.

Blue (indigo). Review the situation through the eyes of the spirit rather than the eyes of the body. Indicates clear thought, imagination, and visualization.

Blue (light blue). Will power, communication, confession of perceived wrong action; the need to speak your truth through the heart.

Boxed in. The individual perceives no choice.

Boxes. Packing; moving; transition has just occurred.

Bread. The need to self-nurture; seeking spiritual knowledge.

Bricks. Building blocks; new things are taking shape.

Buildings. Often represents the soul at work; new job or changing of position within job. Pay attention to ascending rather than descending on stairs or elevator within the structure. Descending means struggle or relearning old lessons.

C

Calendar. Time in months; pay attention to specific month.

Canary, yellow. Desire for inner freedom; soul wants to take flight.

Car. Ability to move forward.

Car accident. Not living in the now; imbalances; front impact: being too much future-oriented; rear impact: living in the past; left side: overly rational approach, not enough heart; right side: ungrounded, racing mind.

Cat. Instincts, instinctual desire, lack of following one's inner guidance.

Castle. House of soul contracts; attention should be given to the overall appearance of the castle (i.e., new, old, good condition, falling apart, strong, etc.), as well as surrounding landscapes. Note location of any needed repair to the bricks and mortar. Foundation: identifies core beliefs. Walls: represent strength. Roof: represents shelter or guidance from above. Drawbridge (down): new information on the way; (up): closed off to new information.

Cheating. Lack of self-esteem and self-worth; gossip; watch and listen for lies being spoken.

Checkers. Strategies are underway to attain a goal.

Climbing mountain. Individual is undergoing intensified soul-growth; important to note climate and weather around the mountain.

Climbing rope. Solo journey upward; individual will see the top.

Cloak. Someone protective is around.

Cloak, black. Someone with a private agenda.

Clouds. Heavenly help; obstacles that can be blown away with certainty and gratitude that all is in cosmic order.

Cloud, dancing. Individual is greatly supported by heaven; time to laugh, play, and dance with your life; celebrate your success.

D

Damsel. Person is seeking rescue. Person will have a strong archetypal influence that identifies their need to be rescued.

Dancing. Need to let go more; playfulness and romance with self or other; often seen around widowed individual. Passed-over loved one wants them to know they can still dance.

Death (coffin and flowers). A physical death is coming or being processed by individual.

Death (gravesite). A symbolic death related to business relationships; part of the person's nature.

Digging. Looking for what is perceived as missing.

Digging, soil. Unearthing core beliefs; preparing for restructure.

Dog. Loyalty; issues pertaining to the need or appreciation of loyalty, or the lack thereof.

Door. Another side, end of cycle, new beginnings; pay attention to age, structure and weight; often represents time periods.

Duck. Seeking order; nurture and self-pampering.

E

Eagle. Clear sight; focused; self-reliant; freedom to soar.

Earth. Global view; global impact; take time to nurture and mother self.

Eyes. Need to look deeper into a situation.

Eye, single. Psychic opening is about to occur; seeing the truth.

Eyes, pair. Looking through the window into the soul.

F

Father. Desire to communicate or heal paternal issues; represents the masculine—the need to do, or take action.

Fence. Desire to have a boundary in place.

Fire. Transformation, purification, and rebirth.

Flag. International move or travel.

Floor. Describes pathway; note whether it is shiny, clean, dirty, rugged, polished, etc.

Flowers. Represent occasions such as weddings and funerals; a particular flower around individual represents gift from loved one. Pay attention to color and face of the flower for specific message.

Forest. A mystical journey; usually individual will be learning the importance of endurance in some area of life.

Foundation. Opportunity for new building, business, or house to be constructed; also indicates core beliefs.

Fountain. Serenity; time to turn within; cleansing; possible salty warm tears of sorrow or clear cool tears of joy.

Frog. Take a leap; emotional cleansing; camouflage.

Furnishings, physical items. Probable move.

G

Garage. Usually indicates the benefits of tinkering or mechanical applications. This image is seen when the individual needs to reassess their purpose or right action; a place of introspection.

Gas wells. Untapped resources; money is coming.

Geese. Time to change direction.

God. Great Orchestrating Design is at work; time to be still.

Gold. God; divine messengers; prosperity; wealth; natural spiritual abundance.

Golf. Strategies are necessary, play against self only; being honest; integrity.

Green. Matters of the heart and healing energies; beauty and deep appreciation

Green light. Go; do not look back.

H

Head in clouds. Person is waiting for things to change or shift; needs grounding.

Horse. Issues around harnessing power; the individual should note whether the horse or the person commands the power in the image. Pay attention to self-esteem, experiences related to self-worth.

Horse eyes. What is being avoided to see; ability to see clearly.

House. Represents the soul.

House, changes. Represents soul changes.

Hurricane. Feeling restless; everything being turned upside down; scattered, disjointed; often represents significant personal growth and change.

I

Incense (being smelled and/or seen). The sacred; time for reflection, shutting down the physical, and opening to the spirit within.

Iris. Spring, softness, and strength.

J

Jackhammer. Breaking up the old foundation; rebuilding.

Joker. Someone is putting on a false face; pay attention to gut-feeling!

𝒦

Key. Opening or unlocking potential and possibility.

King. Royalty; power; influence over others; breaking rules.

Knight. Protection; warrior; justice; a desire for love or romance.

Knocking. Someone living or passed over who wants to give a message.

Knocking, on wood. Individual is not listening, or unaware of guidance coming in.

𝓛

Ladder. A supported climb, yet includes some risk.

Lassoing. Desire to attain or secure something for personal gain.

Leader. Time to take command; having faith in the unknown.

Line. Boundaries; drawing the line.

𝓜

Money (seen as oil, rushing water, green cash, or coins). Prosperity.

Mother. Implies nurturing or need to wean from co-dependent relationship; the power of creative force; intention; when seen on left side of client, maternal side; right side of client, paternal side; usually shows up when support is needed.

Mountain. Growth for the soul; attention should be given to the place where the individual is standing on the mountain, i.e., base, middle, or top.

N

Nest. Home; often seen around mothers of children they are concerned about.

Numbers. Often identifies abilities or struggles in that area; check numerology for in-depth vibration impact when specific numbers are shown.

O

Open doors, windows, and pathways. It is time to proceed.

Orange (color). Need or desire for authentic power and control in reference to relationship and money issues.

Ostrich. Inquisitive; suggests client wants more understanding about key issues.

P

Parent(s). Support is being given or forgiveness is needed. Standing behind: supporting; beside: on left side, indicates mother; on right side, father. When parent seems distant, forgiveness is needed.

Purple. Divine guidance; introspection; Christ Consciousness; unity.

Q

Queen. Royal energies; clients who exude this energy are sometimes misperceived as being arrogant.

R

Rain. Tears; can be either joyous or tears of sadness cleansing the soul. Healing is underway.

Rainbow. A promise will be kept.

Red. Foundation and grounding; review core beliefs, both business and personal.

Rope. Heavenly support; help with pulling out of situation.

Rope, tight. Ability to stay in balance in light of danger.

S

Sand. Shifting or softening of core beliefs; if sand is contained, it identifies a particular area (family, finance, health) is undergoing change.

Singing. Represents the lifting of voices; happiness and expression.

Sun. Things are clear to move forward; you are supported.

T

Teeter-totter. Uncertainty; often indicates individual needs to look at both sides equally; stable or equalized teeter-totter indicates situation is balanced.

Teeth. Representative of person's ability to bite into and digest situation.

Teeth, falling out. Spiritual transformation; concept of self is in transition.

U

Umbrella. Person is being shielded from the rain, or tears of others.

V

Violin. Music that will heal the heart and soothe the mind.

W

Weather. Identifies the emotions and mind clarity around a situation.

White. Indicates all the colors. The color white indicates the overall soul contract information; location indicates the doorway to the guides and teachers of the individual.

Wind. Rushing: confusion and turbulence; softly blowing: cooling and calming.

Y

Yellow. Use of intellect, sense of self, intuition and teaching. Questions individual is asking involve, Who am I? Where do I fit in? What is my purpose?

Z

Zebra. Black-and-white thinking; temper-related issues.

Moreah Ragusa

Moreah Ragusa, RFM, is a psychothera-pist, registered family mediator, mar-riage counselor, divorce coach, corporate and life coach, and a popular keynote speaker. She has been a student and teacher of the internationally respected spiritual text *A Course in Miracles* for more than sixteen years and is recognized for her ability to illuminate and clarify its teachings.

Deeply committed to helping others on their life path, Moreah is the founder and president of The Phoenix Coaching and Transformation Corporation in Calgary, Alberta. The company offers life mastery strategies to reveal each individual's inherent wisdom, prosperity, free-dom, and power.

Moreah is the author of several other books on rela-tionship transformation, including *Rediscovering Your Authentic Self: Applying A Course in Miracles to Everyday Life; The New Mar-riage Paradigm: Inspiring the Transformation and Evolution of Com-mitted Relationships;* and *The New Divorce Paradigm: Transitioning Your Relationship with Integrity.*

Passionate about sharing her deep understanding of spiri-tual truths and the human journey, Moreah has appeared on numerous radio and television shows.

OTHER BOOKS BY MOREAH RAGUSA

The New Marriage Paradigm:
  Inspiring the Transformation and Evolution of
  Committed Relationships

The New Divorce Paradigm:
  Transitioning Your Relationship with Integrity

Rediscovering Your Authentic Self:
  Applying A Course in Miracles to Everyday Life
  Also available on CD in audio book format; abridged

JOURNALS:

The New Marriage Paradigm Journal:
  An Explorative Workbook Designed to Strengthen Your
  Committed Relationship

The New Divorce Paradigm Journal:
  An Explorative Workbook Designed to Support Your Journey
  to Marriage Completion

CDs:

Rediscovering Your Authentic Self:
  Applying A Course in Miracles to Everyday Life
  (audio book; abridged)

Introducing A Course in Miracles

Relationships: Our Journey to Enlightenment

Creating Mastery in Your Life

Understanding A Course in Miracles

Contact Information

To order Moreah's books and CDs, please visit
www.moreahragusa.com

For information on our services, or to book Moreah for
a lecture, conference, seminar, or retreat, please visit
www.thephoenixcoaching.com

E-mail: info@thephoenixcoaching.com
Phone: 403-278-3700

Thank you
Please visit our special Web page at
www.moreahragusa.com/bookgift.htm
to download your free audio gift.
It's our way of saying thank you
for purchasing this book!

Books

REDISCOVERING YOUR AUTHENTIC SELF
Applying A Course in Miracles to Everyday Life

Your soul holds the answers to your deepest questions and nurtures the desires of your authentic heart. When we consciously apply spiritual principles based on love, truth, and forgiveness, we become empowered to tap into our soul's abundant creative power, enabling us to create the life we truly desire. Ancient and modern spiritual teachings all rest upon this truth.

When you reclaim your authentic self, you will –

- Live a life free from seeking the approval of others
- Have the confidence to speak in public
- Look at life as a playful dance, rather than a painful struggle
- Radiate charisma, joy, and confidence
- Be viewed as a someone everyone wants to know
- Increase you natural intuitive abilities
- Have the courage to follow your dreams

THE NEW MARRIAGE PARADIGM

Inspiring the Transformation and Evolution of Committed Relationships

The breakthrough ideas presented in this book define the deepest meaning of success for any marriage. With wisdom and compassion, Moreah Ragusa explains the evolutionary process through which all romantic relationships must advance. At the heart of the book is the author's pulsing desire to help couples establish a more intimate, transparent, and fulfilling union.

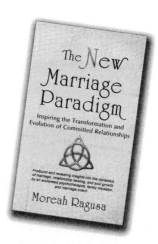

The strategies provided in *The New Marriage Paradigm* will help you to –

- Understand relationship struggles and why they are necessary to your overall personal growth
- Appreciate the impact of value differences and see how our differing priorities and desires run our relationships
- Eliminate the possibility of having infidelity touch your union
- Increase the probability of a mutually fulfilling passionate sexual partnership
- Create workable agreements with regard to disciplining the kids
- Rebuild intimacy, friendship, and trust between you and your mate

THE NEW MARRIAGE PARADIGM JOURNAL

An Explorative Workbook Designed to Strengthen Your Committed Relationship

The powerfully revealing questions and exercises presented in this journal, which can also be used as a stand-alone workbook, will guide you to discover the deepest meaning of success for your marriage. Insights gained from answering these questions will help you discover the hidden fears and motives that identify the reasons for your relationship struggles. Journaling acts like a personal therapist, because we write things we believe that are not necessarily true, but feel true for us, and that consequently "run" the relationship.

Reviewing our emotionally driven thoughts and fears helps us to see which painful memories need addressing and which ones we need to let go of.

THE NEW DIVORCE PARADIGM
Transitioning Your Relationship with Integrity

Drawing on many years of success in helping couples move through the divorce process with mutual respect, Moreah Ragusa offers workable tools to significantly soften the experience of marriage completion.

The breakthrough ideas in this book offer strategies to help you or someone you know learn how to –

- Abolish the fear that accompanies divorce
- Minimize guilt about creating pain for your family members
- Maintain stability for your kids
- Resolve asset division fairly and wisely without lawyers
- Avoid ugly custody fights by having great negotiating skills

The New Divorce Paradigm is a powerful guidebook to building a bridge to new beginnings.

THE NEW DIVORCE PARADIGM JOURNAL
An Explorative Workbook Designed to Support Your Journey to Marriage Completion

The New Divorce Paradigm Journal is designed as an experiential support tool for *The New Divorce Paradigm*, a breakthrough book offered to help divorcing couples transition their relationship with integrity and compassion. In this Journal, you are posed specific questions that will create a framework to support your new life path. When you answer these questions, they become a map that clearly and concisely directs you towards your new life.

Work with this Journal to –

- Set powerful intentions through writing out your future dreams
- Identify and work through fears by applying a day-by-day approach
- Become clear and truthful about where you are strong and courageous
- Keep a record of one of the most transformative, insightful, and life-altering experiences you will ever have.